TOWARD THE PROMISED LAND

FRONTISPIECE   Harriet Tubman (left), legendary "conductor" on the slave escape route known as the Underground Railroad, lines up with a few of those whom she had guided to freedom in the 1850s.

ON THE COVER   Members of an extended slave family gather outside their cabin in early 1861.

Chelsea House Publishers
Editorial Director   Richard Rennert
Executive Managing Editor   Karyn Gullen Browne
Copy Chief   Robin James
Picture Editor   Adrian G. Allen
Creative Director   Robert Mitchell
Art Director   Joan Ferrigno
Production Manager   Sallye Scott

Milestones in Black American History
Senior Editor   Marian W. Taylor
Associate Editor   Margaret Dornfeld
Series Originator and Adviser   Benjamin I. Cohen
Series Consultants   Clayborne Carson, Darlene Clark Hine

Staff for TOWARD THE PROMISED LAND
Editorial Assistant   Sydra Mallery
Designer   Cambraia Magalhães
Picture Researcher   Toby Greenberg

First Printing

1 3 5 7 9 8 6 4 2

Library of Congress Cataloging-in-Publication Data

King, Wilma, 1942–
    Toward the promised land, 1851–1861: from Uncle Tom's cabin to the onset of the Civil War/Wilma King.
        p. cm. — (Milestones in Black American history)
    Includes bibliographical references and index.
        ISBN 0-7910-2265-X
        ISBN 0-7910-2691-4 (pbk.)
    1.Afro-Americans—History—To 1863—Juvenile literature. [1. Afro-Americans—History—To 1863.] I. Title. II. Series.
E185.K47 1995   94-42109
973'.0496073—dc20   CIP
                                                                                            AC

CONTENTS

MILESTONES IN BLACK AMERICAN HISTORY

INTRODUCTION

Toward the Promised Land tells the fascinating story of black America in the years just before the Civil War. By 1851, tension between the slaveholding South and the largely abolitionist (antislavery) North had been simmering for decades. It had risen sharply with the passage of the Compromise of 1850, a law that allowed territories entering the Union to decide if they would be "free" or "slave" states. The compromise's backers hoped it would put a lid on the slavery controversy, but it contained a fatal flaw: the Fugitive Slave Act. This provision not only empowered southern slaveholders to reclaim their runaway black "property" but legally forced northerners to help them do it. Because most northerners applauded the black men and women who fled to freedom, the slave law intensified their loathing of the South and its "peculiar institution." Southerners, in turn, raged against northern interference in their quest for runaways. The Fugitive Slave Act thus accomplished the exact opposite of its designers' intentions: it pushed the nation closer to the great Civil War that would almost destroy it.

Then, into this seething cauldron dropped a bombshell: Harriet Beecher Stowe's Uncle Tom's Cabin. A powerful, emotionally charged 1852 novel about the cruelties of slavery, Uncle Tom played no small part in triggering the bloody conflict between the North and South. (When Stowe called on Abraham Lincoln at the White House, the president reportedly asked, "Is this the little woman whose book made such a great war?")

Free African Americans had mixed reactions to Uncle Tom. Some praised it for its obvious sympathy to the abolitionist cause; others damned it for presenting black men and women as simple beings wholly at the mercy of whites. A number of black critics refuted it by writing their own novels about slavery. America's black literary tradition begins with these writers, who include freeborn abolition-ist and physician Martin R. Delany, author of *Blake; or, the Huts of America*. Twentieth-century scholar Floyd J. Miller has called Blake "the most important black novel of the period and one of the most revealing fictional works ever completed by an African American."

Just as *Uncle Tom* was being published, a tall black woman was shaking the rafters at a Women's Rights Convention in Akron, Ohio. When former slave Sojourner Truth thundered out her celebrated "Ain't I a Woman?" speech, she made history, both for the antislavery movement and for the cause of women's rights. And Truth was not alone: the pre–Civil War decade abounded with brilliant African American orators and writers. Frederick Douglass, a Maryland slave who escaped, educated himself, and became an outstanding editor, author, and speaker, thrilled audiences with his eloquent pleas for emancipation and black education. The list goes on: in this decade, Mary Ann Shadd Cary battled for fugitive rights in Canada, where she also edited a newspaper and wrote countless tracts and books; Frances Ellen Harper, one of the age's most prolific writers and popular poets, published a stream of best-sellers, including *Poems on Miscellaneous Subjects*; Solomon Northup published the widely read *Twelve Years a Slave*.

Meanwhile, the slavery controversy continued to boil. In 1856, militant white abolitionist John Brown triggered a small-scale but savage war by slaughtering five proslavery settlers in what became known as "bleeding Kansas." Brown would finish the decade at the end of a rope, sentenced to death for trying to organize a massive slave breakout at Harpers Ferry, Virginia, in 1859. Adding fuel to the fire was the infamous *Dred Scott* decision, an 1857 U.S. Supreme Court verdict stating that because African Americans were not citizens, they had no legal rights, and were not, in effect, even *people*.

In 1858 Americans avidly followed (by way of newspapers and lectures) the Illinois debates between proslavery senatorial candidate Stephen Douglas and antislavery candidate Abraham Lincoln. The silver-tongued Lincoln lost that election, but he went on to win the U.S. presidency in 1860. Deeply alarmed by his victory, 11 southern states reacted by leaving the Union to form a slavocracy, the Confederate States of America.

Concluding the turbulent prewar years was the sound of artillery: Confederate guns fired on the federal post at Fort Sumter, South Carolina, in April 1861. After a 33-hour battle, Union defenders struck the Star-Spangled Banner, Confederate attackers raised the Stars and Bars, and the sundered nation began four years of bloody fratricide.

From this explosive decade, African America's future took shape. Free northern blacks and their white abolitionist allies joined hands and met their enemy with passion and courage. Powered by their battle cries—and by the silent yearning of millions of enslaved southerners—the nation rolled on, heading toward a world that would promise liberty and justice for *all*.

MILESTONES
1851–1861

1851 • September 11: William Parker, a former slave living in Christiana, Pennsylvania, organizes a rebellion to protect four fugitive slaves from their master. The incident represents the first successful protest of the Fugitive Slave Act of 1850.

1852 • May: Addressing a Women's Rights Convention in Akron, Ohio, former slave Sojourner Truth delivers her powerful "Ain't I a Woman?" speech.

• The Philadelphia, Pennsylvania, Society of Friends opens the Institute for Colored Youth, the first coeducational classical high school for African Americans.

• Harriet Beecher Stowe publishes her antislavery novel, *Uncle Tom's Cabin*, which becomes a driving force behind the abolition movement.

1853 • Prominent black abolitionist Samuel Ringgold Ward launches his newspaper, the *Provincial Freeman*, in Windsor, Canada.

• Solomon Northup publishes his narrative, *Twelve Years a Slave*.

1854 • Ordered to sit in the back of a New York City trolley car, Elizabeth Jennings sues the transportation company for practicing discrimination. The court awards her $225 in damages.

• Frances Ellen Harper publishes *Poems on Miscellaneous Subjects*. Harper also becomes a traveling lecturer on the abolitionist circuit.

• Senator Stephen A. Douglas of Illinois introduces the Kansas-Nebraska Bill, a proposal that would allow settlers to decide whether or not to permit slavery in their territories.

• In reaction to the threat of slavery in the western territories, abolitionist northerners form a new organization: the Republican party.

• Anthony Burns, a fugitive Virginia slave, is reclaimed by his master in Boston, Massachusetts, and returned to slavery, a major defeat for northern abolitionists.

1856
- Militant abolitionist John Brown revenges the murder of five antislavery men in Kansas by killing five proslavery settlers. The bloodletting sets off a chain of violence in which 200 people are killed.

- James Buchanan, who promises not to interfere with slavery in the territories, is elected president of the United States.

1857
- The U.S. Supreme Court rules (in *Scott v. Sanford*) that Missouri slave Dred Scott did not gain his freedom by living with his master in the free state of Illinois. As a slave, says the court, Scott is a citizen neither of Missouri nor of the United States, and has no civil rights. The decision moves the nation closer to civil war.

1858
- Republican presidential candidate Abraham Lincoln challenges his opponent, Stephen A. Douglas, to seven debates. The verbal duels make Lincoln famous for his eloquent antislavery views, but they do not win him this election.

1859
- John Brown leads a small force of men against the federal arsenal at Harpers Ferry, Virginia. The effort fails, and Brown is hanged.

- Martin R. Delany, a prominent black physician, editor, and Underground Railroad agent, publishes *Blake; or the Huts of America,* his response to *Uncle Tom's Cabin.* Delany will later become the first black to be named a major in the Union army.

- Harriet E. Wilson publishes *Our Nig; or, Sketches from the Life of a Free Black,* the first novel written by an African American woman in the United States.

1860
- Abraham Lincoln wins the presidential election.

1861
- Following the lead of South Carolina, the states of Alabama, Florida, Georgia, Louisiana, Mississippi, and Texas break from the United States to form a new nation, the Confederate States of America.

- April 12: Confederate forces open fire on Fort Sumter, a federal garrison in the harbor of Charleston, South Carolina. After a fierce, 33-hour battle, the Union commander surrenders, and the nation is at war.

1

"AIN'T I A WOMAN?"

THE crowd let out a torrent of boos and hisses as a tall, gaunt, dark-skinned woman rose from her seat and walked slowly toward the podium. On this May afternoon in 1852, the second day of the Women's Rights Convention, hundreds of men and women had gathered inside an Akron, Ohio, church to hear authorities from around the nation discuss "the woman question." The speaker they were about to hear was a newcomer to the women's movement, and many of the conventioneers disapproved of her participation. The chair of the meeting, Francis D. Gage, had been told not to allow her to speak, but Gage believed the woman had something important to offer and asked the audience to welcome her. The audience watched the woman take her place as the noise slowly subsided. "Well, children, where there is so much racket," the speaker began, "there must be something out of kilter." In a soft, low voice she continued, "I think that 'twixt de negroes of the South and the

Rights activist Sojourner Truth surveys the world with a characteristically skeptical expression. Born into bondage in New York about 1798, Truth gained her freedom when the state abolished slavery in 1828.

Truth's stern visage greets readers of her 1853 Narrative, the autobiography she dictated to a friend. Although she could not read or write, Truth was exceptionally witty and articulate.

women at the North, all talking about rights, the white men will be in a fix pretty soon."

With these words Sojourner Truth, a former slave from Hurley, New York, launched a speech that drew together the common threads of two of the 19th century's most prominent reform movements. As an antislavery feminist, Truth had often appeared on programs with William Lloyd Garrison, editor of the abolitionist paper the *Liberator*, and the slave-born Frederick Douglass, who later became an internationally known abolitionist. Truth had a reputation as a powerful speaker, but because she was associated with the abolitionist movement, the organizers of the Women's Rights Convention feared her presence would do more harm than good. One woman worried that the nation's newspapers would interpret her partici-

pation as mixing "the abolition and niggers" with the women's cause.

By the time Truth took her place at the podium, several speakers had already gone before her, some supporting equal rights for women, others opposing them. One prominent clergyman had argued that, as women were intellectually inferior to men—a common view in 19th-century America—they did not deserve equal treatment under the law. Sojourner Truth, who had never learned to read or write, was unimpressed by this reasoning. "As for intellect," she remarked, "if a woman have a pint and man a quart, why can't she have her little pint full? You need not be afraid to give us our rights for fear we will take too much. We can't take more than our pint will hold."

Another clergyman had argued that women were the weaker sex and could not be trusted with equal rights. As a child of slavery and a victim of forced manual labor, Sojourner Truth drew on personal experience to refute his argument. "That man over

Suffragist Elizabeth Cady Stanton presides over the first Women's Rights Convention, held in Seneca Falls, New York, in 1848. Attended by 300 women, the event paved the way for the U.S. women's reform movement.

A passionate abolitionist, former slave Frederick Douglass was also an unswerving supporter of women's rights, which he called identical with those of men.

there," she said, referring to the minister, "says that women needs to be helped into carriages and lifted over ditches and to have the best place everywhere." She knew that when the preacher made these remarks, he was referring to white women. No one had helped the strong and muscular Truth into carriages or given her special treatment on account of her "feminine weakness." As if confused, Truth peered at the audience. "And ain't I a woman?" she asked.

Murmurs rippled through the audience. Without waiting for an answer, Truth told her listeners that she had "ploughed, and planted, and gathered [crops] into barns" just as men had. Truth had endured whippings; she had borne 13 children, and she had seen most of them sold away. No one had shielded her from the physical and emotional assaults of slavery. Truth recalled the pain she had suffered and her cries for mercy as her children were taken from her. "None but Jesus heard me," she remembered. "And ain't I a woman?"

Like waves against the shore, Truth's provocative question—"And ain't I a woman?"—kept returning, striking at the soul of her spellbound audience. Sojourner Truth did not see herself as a member of the weaker sex. Nor did she believe that she or any other woman was entitled to anything less than the rights enjoyed by men. Years after she delivered her fiery speech, Gage remembered:

> [Sojourner Truth] had taken us up in her strong arms and carried us safely over the slough of difficulty, turning the whole tide in our favor. I have never in my life seen anything like the magical influence that subdued the mobbish spirit of the day, and turned the sneers and jeers of an excited crowd into notes of respect and admiration.

Sojourner Truth, the only African American woman present at the 1852 Women's Rights Convention, had saved the day.

After this success, Truth continued to give public addresses about rights for women and freedom for African Americans, two topics that were very much a part of the national reform agenda in the early 1850s. As the decade progressed, the "woman question" and the slavery issue became more and more intertwined, for white women who wished to help enslaved blacks wondered how they could do so when their own

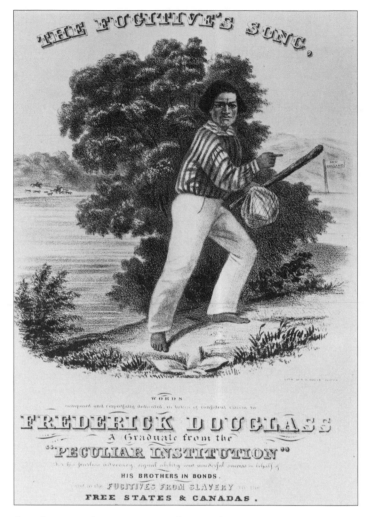

The image of Frederick Douglass adorns sheet music for a popular ballad, "The Fugitive's Song." The escaped slave's courage and dignity, along with his tireless efforts to end the "peculiar institution," made him a hero to many Americans.

freedom and power were limited.

Frederick Douglass, one of the nation's most outspoken abolitionists, had attended the first women's rights convention, which took place July 19, 1848, at Seneca Falls, New York, and championed woman suffrage. On October 30, 1851, Douglass explained:

> In our eyes, the rights of woman and the rights of man are identical—We ask no rights, we advocate no rights for ourselves, which we would not ask and advocate for women. . . . The rights of man and the rights of woman are one and inseparable, and stand upon the same indestructible basis.

Douglass's declaration came a few weeks after one of the most controversial racial conflicts of the decade. On the morning of September 11, 1851, a former slave named William Parker became the center of a violent dispute over the protection of escaped slaves. Parker, who lived in Christiana, Pennsylvania, woke up that day to hear Edward Gorsuch, a Maryland slaveowner, shouting threats outside the door. Gorsuch had come with his son and five other armed whites, including Deputy U.S. Marshal Henry S. Kline, to retrieve four fugitive slaves who, they believed, had taken shelter with Parker, a well-known abettor of runaways.

Gorsuch's slaves had left his plantation the previous winter, and by the terms of the Fugitive Slave Act of 1850, Gorsuch had a legal right to pursue them. Kline carried warrants for their arrest. "You have my property," Gorsuch shouted as he pounded on Parker's door. Parker let him in and, pointing to the beds, bureau, and chairs, invited him to look around the house to see if any of the furnishings belonged to him. He then asked Gorsuch to go into the barn where he kept his hogs and cows. "See if any of them are yours," he said.

According to his own account, which appeared in the March 1866 *Atlantic Monthly*, Parker was ready to "fight until death" to protect the fugitives, whom he was indeed hiding. Working with several other blacks in the area, he had formed an organization to protect escaped slaves. One of its members was his brother-in-law, Alexander Pinckney, who panicked when Gorsuch and his men demanded the fugitives; Parker threatened to "blow out" his brains if he surrendered.

While Parker distracted the raiding party, his wife blew a horn to signal for assistance. In response, dozens of men, black and white, hastened to the scene with guns, swords, and other weapons. The crowd made Kline nervous, but the elderly Gorsuch was

William Lloyd Garrison, publisher of the abolitionist newspaper the Liberator *and founder of the influential New England Anti-Slavery Society, never minced words. "He that is with the slave," he said, "is against the slaveholder."*

determined to recapture his "property." As he and his son walked toward the barn, Parker and his companions followed. Catching sight of the blacks, Kline and the other whites fled; in the turmoil that followed, Gorsuch was killed and his son seriously wounded. Neighbors quickly notified federal officials, who dispatched 50 marines to Christiana, but by the time they arrived, the fighting was over and the four fugitives had disappeared.

Parker and two of his colleagues fled north to Rochester, New York, where Frederick Douglass, who had escaped bondage 13 years earlier, gave them food and shelter. Douglass described the men as heroes who had defended themselves against "mansteallers and murderers." Parker later went on to Canada, where his wife eventually joined him.

The government, meanwhile, pressed charges against 40 of the men involved in the Christiana battle, but only one, Castner Hanway, a local white Quaker, stood trial. Hanway had taken no direct action against Gorsuch, but he had refused to help Kline prevent the attack. The jury acquitted him, and the district attorney sought no further indictments. Parker and his friends had successfully challenged the Fugitive Slave Act of 1850.

Reactions to the Christiana incident varied. Southern newspapers denounced it and Gorsuch's death as "diabolical" and "vile," and some northern newspapers echoed them. Other northern journals praised the fugitives for fighting for their own liberty.

The response to the Christiana episode reflected one of the central debates dividing the North and South in the mid-19th century. After the Revolutionary War, the northern states had either abolished slavery or made provisions to do so. By contrast, slavery had remained steadfast in the South as cotton cultivation spread throughout the region. Although the majority of southern whites were not slaveholders in 1850, most southerners believed that slaveholders' rights should be protected. In the North, meanwhile, many orators, philanthropists, and political leaders argued that slavery should be abolished immediately throughout the nation. By the 1850s there were many northern-based abolitionist organizations, such as the American Anti-Slavery Society, founded in 1833, dedicated to ending slavery.

The philosophical arguments for and against slavery stressed either the personal rights of the

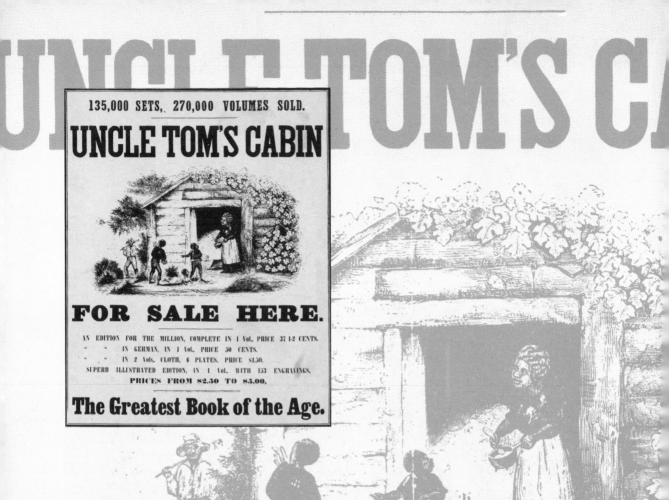

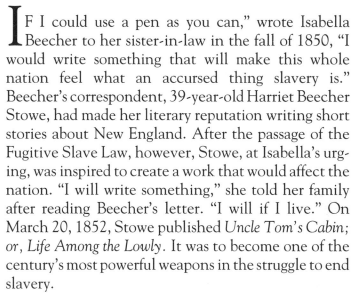

2

UNCLE TOM'S CABIN AND THE POWER OF THE PEN

IF I could use a pen as you can," wrote Isabella Beecher to her sister-in-law in the fall of 1850, "I would write something that will make this whole nation feel what an accursed thing slavery is." Beecher's correspondent, 39-year-old Harriet Beecher Stowe, had made her literary reputation writing short stories about New England. After the passage of the Fugitive Slave Law, however, Stowe, at Isabella's urging, was inspired to create a work that would affect the nation. "I will write something," she told her family after reading Beecher's letter. "I will if I live." On March 20, 1852, Stowe published *Uncle Tom's Cabin; or, Life Among the Lowly*. It was to become one of the century's most powerful weapons in the struggle to end slavery.

As many as 5,000 copies of the novel sold during its first few days in print. By June the book was selling at a rate of 10,000 copies per week. American sales had reached 150,000 by October and more than

The best-selling Uncle Tom's Cabin *increased northern hostility to the South and helped push the nation toward civil conflict. On meeting author Harriet Beecher Stowe in 1862, President Abraham Lincoln reportedly asked, "Is this the little woman who made such a great war?"*

25

The slave Eliza, a leading character in Uncle Tom's Cabin, *prepares to flee with her son Harry after she learns he is to be sold. The novel's deluxe edition carried 153 similar illustrations.*

300,000 by the end of the year. *Uncle Tom's Cabin* was easily the best-selling novel of the 19th century; since its first day of publication, it has never been out of print.

Of the white authors who reached a wide audience in the mid-19th century, only Harriet Beecher Stowe addressed an issue of central importance to African Americans. Born in Litchfield, Connecticut, in 1811, Stowe was the daughter of the prominent clergyman Lyman Beecher. In 1832, when Beecher became president of Lane Theological Seminary, the family moved to Cincinnati, Ohio, where they remained for the next 18 years.

While living with her family near the seminary, Harriet Beecher came face to face with many of the central issues of the slavery debate. Cincinnati's Ohio River marked a boundary between slaveholding and free states, and fugitives fleeing across the river sometimes found their way to the seminary, where Lyman Beecher's students sheltered them. Harriet Beecher also learned about the lives of those in bondage from conversations with the free black women who worked in her father's household.

These experiences eventually found expression in *Uncle Tom's Cabin*, a moral invective against the institution of slavery. The novel begins as a Kentucky plantation owner decides to offset mounting debts by selling two of his slaves, the pious Uncle Tom and a young boy named Harry. As the story progresses, readers see Eliza, Harry's mother, preventing the sale of her son by running away with him, fleeing northward and receiving help along the way. She and her son are eventually reunited with her husband. Meanwhile, a slave trader buys Tom and carries him into the Deep South, where he suffers physical abuse and dies without ever seeing his family again.

The African American response to *Uncle Tom's Cabin* was mixed. William J. Wilson, a regular contributing editor to *Frederick Douglass' Paper*, a popular antislavery journal of the day, wondered whether a "white writer [could] do 'faithful' justice to the black experience of slavery." William G. Allen, a teacher who wrote to the paper, praised *Uncle Tom's Cabin*, but he was less than satisfied with the portrayal of the passive Uncle Tom. "There should be resistance to tyrants," wrote Allen, "if it need be, to the death." Some free black northerners regarded the novel as a godsend, believing that it would gain white sympathy for the antislavery fight at a critical time.

Stowe's most vocal supporter among African Americans was Frederick Douglass. From 1852 to 1853 Douglass published reviews, articles, and comments about *Uncle Tom's Cabin* in his paper. In April 1853 Douglass visited Stowe at her home in Andover, Massachusetts, where the two spent hours discussing education for free African Americans, one of Douglass's most cherished causes.

A few weeks earlier, Douglass had published an article entitled "Learn Trades or Starve!" arguing that blacks could gain greater economic independence if they were given the opportunity to perfect useful skills. Many white tradespeople, Douglass pointed out, objected to training African American apprentices. "Where are the antislavery milliners and seamstresses that will take colored girls," Douglass asked, "and teach them trades, by which they can obtain an honorable living?" Douglass believed that if blacks could acquire trade skills, they would be able to compete with the immigrants who were usually hired before them.

Stowe had promoted black education in *Uncle Tom's Cabin*, and Douglass was confident that her interest in helping African Americans blended with his own. "The Chief good which we anticipate from Mrs. Stowe's mission," he wrote after his April meeting with the author, "is the founding of an INSTITU-

Uncle Tom's Cabin author Harriet Beecher Stowe sits for a portrait about 1870, 20 years after publishing her powerful novel. When congratulated for her literary feat, Stowe sometimes denied authorship: "God wrote it," she would insist.

TION, in which our oppressed and proscribed youth, MALE and FEMALE" might gain trade skills. Stowe had been invited to tour the British Isles, and Douglass hoped that she would use this opportunity to raise money for a black trade school. Douglass continued to print articles on the subject throughout the spring and summer of 1853.

Douglass's association with Stowe eventually sparked a debate between the abolitionist leader and a former colleague, Martin R. Delany. A multitalented man, Delany had been editor of his own newspaper, the *Mystery*, from 1843 to 1847. Later he became coeditor of the *North Star*, a paper Douglass founded in 1847. Delany objected to the notion of African Americans putting themselves in what he called the "fostering care" of whites or relying upon whites for the elevation of the race. The main target of Delany's criticism, however, was not so much Stowe's philanthropy as her sympathy for a white-run organization called the American Colonization Society (ACS). Founded in 1817, the ACS asserted that free blacks could never live in peaceful equality with whites in the United States, and that their best course was to leave the country. In 1822 the ACS established the West African colony Liberia as a home for emigrating African Americans.

Advocates of emigration included white slaveholders who hoped to prevent interaction between free and enslaved blacks, which they believed inspired slaves to seek their own liberty. Some southern African Americans, tired of struggling to make a life for themselves as free men and women in a land that spurned them, were swayed by the ideas put forth by the ACS, but blacks in the North almost universally objected to the idea of colonization. By the 1850s,

Martin R. Delany, the first African American to be named a major in the Union army, was also a skilled physician, a daring Underground Railroad agent, and an accomplished novelist and editor. He strongly opposed African colonization for blacks, instead favoring voluntary black resettlement in Central America.

most African Americans thought of the United States as their homeland, and the idea of "returning" to Africa, the land of their ancestors, held little appeal for them. Those who had enslaved relatives and friends were especially reluctant to follow the course prescribed by the ACS. Others resisted the ACS because they resented its leadership—white people who took charge of matters that affected African Americans without regard for what blacks wanted for themselves.

African American leaders who spoke and wrote on the subject often made a distinction between colonization and emigration. Whereas most blacks objected to colonization programs—relocation efforts initiated by organizations outside the black community—the idea of voluntary emigration gained wider support.

Both Frederick Douglass and Martin Delany opposed colonization. Harriet Beecher Stowe, on the other hand, had shown leanings toward the movement. In fact, one of the characters in *Uncle Tom's Cabin*, George, an ex-fugitive who has received an education at a French university, eventually decides to emigrate to Liberia. George exults as he prepares to leave:

> I go to *my country*,—my chosen, my glorious Africa!—and to her, in my heart, I sometimes apply those splendid words of prophecy: 'Whereas thou hast been forsaken and hated, so that no man went through thee; *I* will make thee an external excellence, a joy of many generations!'

Clearly, Stowe's character has no reservations about the prospect of colonizing Africa.

Delany was wary of Stowe's attitude toward the colonization project; his own aim was not to organize an escape for African Americans but to improve black life in America. If blacks were to emigrate, in Delany's view, they would be better off setting up a new life in

Central or South America rather than in Liberia, a colony he regarded as "a poor *miserable mockery*—a burlesque on a government."

Delany was not alone in criticizing this aspect of Stowe's thinking. The abolitionists Charles B. Ray and George T. Downing, members of the American and Foreign Anti-Slavery Society in New York, regretted Stowe's decision to send her only rebellious male character to Africa. One writer to a black newspaper remarked, "Death or banishment is our doom, say the Slaveocrats, the Colonizationists, and, save the mark—Mrs. Stowe!!"

Scholar Robert S. Levine has suggested that Delany was critical of Douglass's association with Stowe not only because *Uncle Tom's Cabin* supported colonization but because his own book, *The Condition, Elevation, Emigration and Destiny of the Colored People of the United States Politically Considered*, received little attention in *Frederick Douglass's Paper*. *The Condition*, a carefully drafted theoretical study of African Americans, appeared the same year as Stowe's celebrated novel. Levine considers it the most significant book on black nationalism in the 19th century. Like many black leaders who came in his wake, Delany believed that the experience of exploitation shared by people of African descent could serve as a basis for solidarity and a starting point for self-directed progress. "Every person," Delany wrote, "should be the originators of their own destiny, the projectors of their own schemes, and the creators of the events that lead to their destiny." *The Condition* put Delany at odds with black and white abolitionists, and he eventually withdrew it from circulation.

The debate between Delany and Douglass ended inconclusively. Meanwhile, Stowe seemed to lose interest in the educational program she had discussed with Douglass. She raised $535, which she gave to Douglass for his personal use instead of donating a

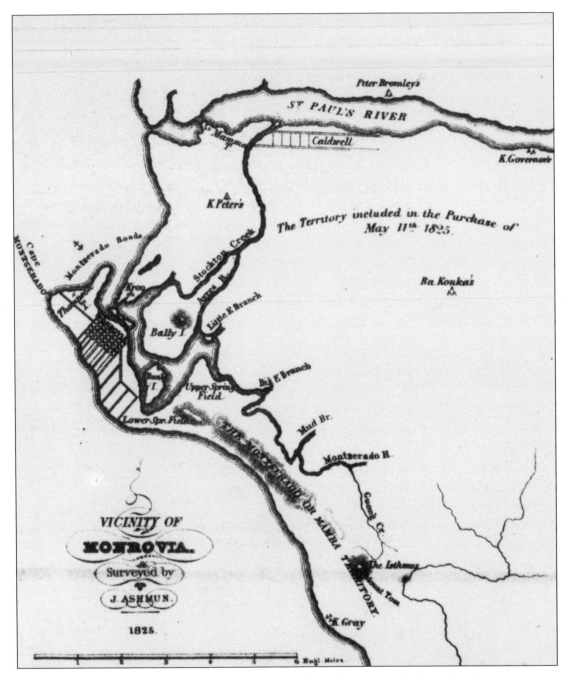

Printed in 1825, a map of the "Vicinity of Monrovia" shows the parcel of land purchased by the white-run American Colonization Society. By the 1860s, 13,000 freeborn blacks and former slaves had moved to the African territory, today the black republic of Liberia.

large sum for the construction of a vocational school. Douglass did not complain. He went on believing that "the name of Harriet Beecher Stowe can never die while the love of freedom lives in the world."

Delany continued to resent Stowe for interpreting the experience of slavery without ever having shared it, and he began writing a novel of his own. In 1859, in the *Anglo-African* magazine, he published the first seven installments of *Blake; or, the Huts of America*, a book with a plot, characters, and dialogue that contrasted sharply with those of *Uncle Tom's Cabin*.

Floyd J. Miller, who edited *Blake; or, the Huts of America* in 1970, considers it the "most important black novel of the period and one of the most revealing fictional works ever completed by an African American." Its main character, Henrico Blacus, or Blake, is a slave who plans a rebellion after his wife is sold and taken to Cuba. The second part of the novel shows Blacus leaving the United States and becoming a general among revolutionaries planning the overthrow of the Cuban government. In writing the novel, Delany incorporated personal experiences, contemporary issues, and themes drawn from slave narratives.

Blake; or, the Huts of America never reached the wide audience Delaney may have hoped for, but as one of the earliest African American novels, it helped launch a rich literary tradition that has continued to flower to the present day. Meanwhile, for all its shortcomings, *Uncle Tom's Cabin* continued to carry out its mission: to "awaken sympathy and feeling" for those who were enslaved, and so to win thousands over to the abolitionist cause.

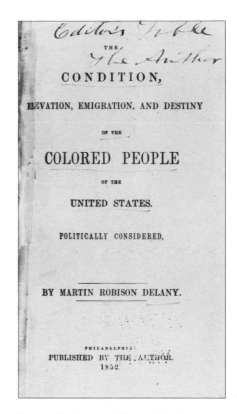

Martin Delany's 1852 study of African Americans unleashed a storm of controversy. Insisting that people of color should master their destiny independent of whites, Delany came under attack by abolitionists of both races.

3

THE ROAD TO INDEPENDENCE

AS long as the U.S. Constitution protected the rights of southern slaveholders, blacks throughout the country continued to face an uncertain future. In response, many looked to Canada, the northernmost stop on the Underground Railroad, as a refuge from oppression. In the first three months after the passage of the Fugitive Slave Act, an estimated 1,000 African Americans per month fled to Canada. By 1860 an additional 12,000 had followed them. Because the 1850 law did not allow persons accused of running away to testify on their own behalf, free blacks, as well as runaways, were subject to capture and sale into bondage. In some courts, officials received $10 when they authorized a fugitive's return and only $5 when they determined that the person in question was not a fugitive.

A 1790 census placed the number of free blacks in the United States at 59,466; by 1850 this figure had increased to 434,449. The growth in the free black

Former slaves—Anne Mary Jane Hunt, Mansfield Smith, Lucinda Seymour (left to right, standing), Henry Stevenson, and Bush Johnson—gather for a portrait in Windsor, Ontario. Like thousands of other blacks, the quintet had fled to Canada to avoid prosecution under the 1850 Fugitive Slave Act.

Mary Ann Shadd Cary, a freeborn African American teacher and journalist who settled in Canada, alienated many aid-society officials with her tough-minded views: blacks, she asserted, needed not financial help but the chance to become self-sufficient citizens.

population can be attributed largely to childbirth, for children born to free women enjoyed the same status as their mothers. Before their deaths, slaveholders also sometimes manumitted, or legally freed, their servants or made provisions for manumission in their wills. Skilled slaves occasionally earned enough money to purchase their own freedom or that of family members. When the Fugitive Slave Act was passed, nearly half of America's free blacks lived in the North, and it was there that the majority of the fugitive cases were heard. In order to avoid the threat of bondage, in the 1850s many free African Americans chose to leave

America behind and settle with black fugitives in Canada. Among Canada's better-known black residents was Henry Bibb, a slave-born Kentuckian who fled the United States in 1850 and founded the *Voice of the Fugitive* in 1851.

Another influential journalist, Mary Ann Shadd, moved to Canada in 1851. Born in Wilmington, Delaware, to a prominent free black family, Shadd was the oldest of 13 children. Her father, Abraham Shadd, was a subscription agent for William Lloyd Garrison's *Liberator* and used his home as an Underground Railroad station. As a child, Mary Ann dreamed of becoming an active leader in the abolitionist movement. Inspired by her father's association with the *Liberator*, she grew up to become an investigative reporter and newspaper editor.

African Americans could learn about Canada from *Notes on Canada West*, a 44-page pamphlet Shadd published in 1852. In it, Shadd argued that Canada's weather, landscape, and "beneficial political climate" made it a more favorable location for African Americans wishing to emigrate than any other place. Shadd explained that in Canada whites had no legal right to discriminate against blacks. Tavern owners and boat operators sometimes refused service to African Americans, she wrote, but those who suffered mistreatment of this kind could receive legal redress. Shadd also gave a positive appraisal of Canada's churches and schools.

Apart from writing, one of Shadd's main concerns was the welfare of the fugitive slaves who had found refuge near her home in Windsor, Ontario. The refugee community in Canada was burdened by inadequate housing, illiteracy, poverty, and poor health. Shadd had taught school in New Jersey and New York, and she decided to open her own educational facility in Canada. Believing that segregation limited opportunities for African Americans, she set out to make

One of many escaped slaves who described their experiences in print, Henry Bibb published his Narrative *in 1849. After emigrating to Canada, the Kentucky-born author started an abolitionist newspaper,* Voice of the Fugitive.

her school integrated, thus coming into conflict with other immigrants to Canada, especially Henry Bibb and his wife, Mary. The Bibbs believed that living in separate communities from whites gave blacks a chance to prove that they could succeed on their own.

The conflict between Shadd and the Bibbs came to a head when Shadd, who was having difficulty collecting school fees, received a $125 donation from the American Missionary Society (AMS). Fearing that tuition payments would stop if parents knew she had another source of income, Shadd did not make the grant known to the public. Four months later, Bibb learned of the AMS donation and published an article about it in his newspaper. Shadd was dismissed by the AMS shortly after the story appeared.

Wasting no time in brooding over the school's failure, however, Shadd decided to help the community in a different way, working for an antislavery paper called the *Provincial Freeman*. The paper, which bore the motto "Self-Reliance Is the True Road to Independence," was launched in 1853 by the prominent black abolitionist Samuel Ringgold Ward. According to an article printed in the second issue, its purpose was to keep the 40,000 African Americans in Canada informed about local activities and events in the United States and to tell readers in the United States about their kinsmen in Canada.

Shadd's official title was business manager. She solicited subscribers for the *Provincial Freeman* while touring Canada and the United States to speak against slavery and in favor of emigration. During her visit to Philadelphia in 1855, friends of the paper organized a fund-raiser for her at Shilo Church during which Elizabeth Taylor Greenfield, the first African American to earn an international reputation as a singer, performed. Greenfield, who was called the "Black Swan," included antislavery songs in her repertoire.

Although Ward was the paper's official editor, he was often too busy with his own speaking engagements to oversee the journal's publication, and much of the work fell to Shadd. Aware of public opposition to women working at "men's jobs," at first she signed her articles with initials instead of her full name. In an 1856 editorial, however, Frederick Douglass confirmed that Shadd was thoroughly capable of handling her position. He wrote:

> This lady, with very little assistance from others, has sustained *The Provincial Freeman* for more than two years. She has had to contend with lukewarmness, false friends, open

enemies, ignorance and small pecuniary means. The tone of her paper has been at times harsh and complaining and whatever may be thought or felt of this we are bound to bear testimony to the unceasing industry, the unconquerable zeal and commendable ability which she has shown. We do not know her equal among the colored ladies of the United States.

The *Provincial Freeman* took its own position on the day's issues, criticizing advocates of segregation and ridiculing the AMS's Refugee Home Society. The AMS's aim was to obtain and sell land to immigrants at reasonable prices, and to help them meet their needs through schools and churches. However well-intentioned, the organization met with limited success: in 1852 only 22 families lived in the homes it provided. Shadd believed the society received enough funds to give immigrants free land, and she also disapproved of the way it distributed clothing to fugitives. The *Provincial Freeman* treated the Anti-Slavery Society of Canada little better; the newspaper heaped scorn on the society for its allegedly snobbish air and its officials' imperious attitudes.

Through the *Provincial Freeman*, Shadd waged an "anti-begging" campaign against agents who solicited money to help support Canadian immigrants. Shadd maintained that newly arrived fugitives needed assistance and were grateful for the help, but that after their initial period of adjustment, they were better off supporting themselves. Providing them with money, she argued, undermined their chances of becoming a self-sufficient community.

In attacking the AMS, the Anti-Slavery Society, and other institutions, Shadd used language that 19th-century readers considered inappropriate for a woman. Describing her opponents with such caustic phrases as "moral pest," "petty despot," and "moral monster," she startled the more conservative members of black society even as she kept subscribers reading.

But despite its sharp tone and biting criticism, the *Provincial Freeman* provided its readers with a vital link between African Americans in Canada and the United States.

African Americans who wanted to emigrate had other options than Canada: refugee communities also existed in Mexico, Haiti, South America, and Liberia. Of these sites, Liberia was the most popular. Henry Highland Garnet, an African American abolitionist who regarded emigration as an effective path to wealth and power, predicted that Liberia would "become the Empire State of Africa." The immigrants to Liberia included freeborn blacks, manumitted slaves, and Africans freed from slave ships operating in violation of an 1808 ban on the overseas slave trade. Slavers who were apprehended had to give up their human cargoes. The American and British navies patrolled the seas to stop ships illegally transporting Africans to the Western Hemisphere. Between 1841 and 1857 the British kept an average of 18 vessels patrolling the seas for slave ships; the U.S. Navy maintained four patrol ships with the same mission during that period.

The American Colonization Society ran a successful publicity campaign, contrasting the hardships of black life in the United States with the opportunities for freedom in Liberia. The ACS sponsored 147 ships carrying 18,959 passengers to Liberia between 1817 and 1865. For each person transported to Liberia by the ACS, the society received more than 10 inquiries about the West African nation.

The Reverend Henry Highland Garnett helped found the African Civilization Society, an American organization with two goals: to dispel the myths of African inferiority associated with enslavement and to persuade African Americans to move to Africa.

The Liberian population had reached nearly 20,000 in the 1860s. Of that number, the United States supplied some 13,000, nearly 30 percent of whom were freeborn blacks who had decided to emigrate entirely on their own. For recaptured Africans and manumitted slaves, however, emigration was generally arranged by an outside partner. Newly freed families rarely had the resources to carry out such a

plan on their own, but with the aid of the ACS, owners sometimes emancipated their bondservants and sent them to Liberia. Elizabeth Greenfield's owner, for example, freed the singer's family to emigrate to Liberia in 1821.

Recaptured Africans made up only 6 percent of Liberia's population until 1846. Later this number increased greatly; in 1860, following an abrupt increase in illegal slave traffic, more than 4,000 Africans were sent to Liberia. The Liberian government created a special committee to help settle the large number of newcomers. In addition, in 1860 the U.S. government agreed to provide the ACS with a year's worth of aid for each repatriated African. It paid $100 for each African over eight years of age and $50 for younger children. Not all of the recaptured Africans wanted to remain in Liberia, and many of them tried to make their way back to their places of birth.

Massachusetts senator Edward Everett addresses an 1853 meeting of the American Colonization Society in Washington, D.C. Deeply conservative, Everett backed black emigration to Liberia largely because it would remove blacks from American society.

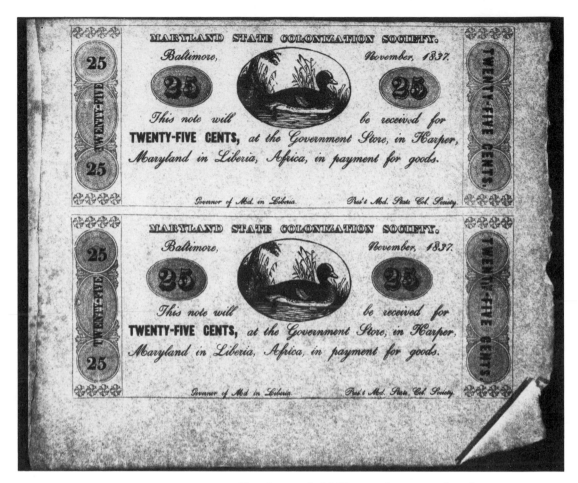

The Maryland State Coloniza-
tion Society issued this scrip
(a document good for purchases)
in 1837. Given to African
Americans interested in making
their homes in Liberia, the
scrip was paid for out of
donations to the society.

By the mid-1850s, enthusiasm for the emigration movement had decreased sharply. Most African Americans were too poor to pay for their own passage to Liberia, and many simply preferred to try to achieve freedom at home. In 1855 the National Convention of Colored Men in Philadelphia received a letter favoring colonization. When a member suggested returning the letter, abolitionist George T. Downing moved that it be burned to save the cost of a three-cent stamp.

Meanwhile, settlers in Liberia set up a society that mirrored what they had known in America. Those who were freeborn, better educated, and more prosperous, held leadership positions. Those who had come to Liberia as emancipated slaves usually worked as farmers or traders. Craftsmen also found work in the building trades, and in 1859, they organized a union. Carpenters earned salaries of 50 to 75 cents per day; masons received $1 a day for their labor; supervisors or "head workmen" received $3 per day.

Liberians of every social rank enjoyed religious activities and other friendly gatherings. A group of men established the first independent Masonic order in 1851, and other fraternal orders and benevolent societies soon followed. The Baptists, Methodist Episcopalians, and Presbyterians received a steady flow of converts. Churchgoing women might belong to the Daughters of Temperance or the Sisters of Friendship.

Although they enjoyed greater opportunities in Liberia, most African American immigrants found it difficult to adjust to a new continent and to leave their memories of America behind. "Nothing could afford me more pleasure," wrote Matilda Skipwith to her former owner, "than to visit again the scenes of childhood & look upon those faces which were once familiar to me." John Hartwell Cocke had emancipated Skipwith and other members of her family in 1833. Her letters attest to the pain endured by thousands of African Americans who left their homeland for Africa's shores, hoping to find the freedom, dignity, and prosperity America had denied them.

4

THE COLOR LINE

AFRICAN Americans of the 19th century experienced life differently, depending on whether they were enslaved or free, male or female. The status of free blacks lay somewhere between that of their enslaved contemporaries and that of whites; although they enjoyed many of the rights guaranteed white citizens, they faced many economic, social, and political limitations unknown to whites.

Most free blacks carried certificates of freedom in order to defend themselves against abduction and enslavement. *Twelve Years a Slave*, a narrative published in 1853, describes the abduction, enslavement, and rescue of a free black named Solomon Northup. By 1855 this compelling account had sold 27,000 copies and persuaded many readers to support abolition. Until the Civil War free blacks continued to live in fear of losing their status and living the remainder of their days in bondage.

An 1854 poster urges all opponents of "slave-catchers" to unite in thwarting these "executors of the Kidnapping Act of 1850." Horrified by the Fugitive Slave Act, many northerners felt justified in violating it.

To be sure, free blacks enjoyed some legal rights. They could sue and be sued, and they could testify in court against other African Americans. They could not, however, testify against whites. The law recognized the marriages of free blacks, who could also own property; in 1860 free black Virginians owned more than 60 thousand acres of land. In the same year, free black Marylanders paid taxes on more than $1 million in real estate; property owned by free blacks in North Carolina and South Carolina ran into the hundreds of thousands of dollars. The value of property among free blacks in Louisiana exceeded $15 million in 1860.

A small number of free African Americans also owned slaves. Two hundred ninety-seven black slaveholders in South Carolina owned a total of 1,277 slaves in 1850. In some cases, these slaves were family members, held by their relatives to avoid laws requiring manumitted blacks to move out of the state. But other blacks owned bondservants for the same reason that whites owned them: to help them get richer. William "April" Ellison, for example, was a former slave who purchased his freedom in 1816. After becoming a wealthy cotton planter and manufacturer of cotton gins, Ellison owned as many as 63 slaves. The women and children worked in his fields and produced the food for the household, and the men and boys worked in the machine shop.

In looking for nonfarm work, free blacks ran into almost universal discrimination. White artisans, often unwilling to compete with skilled African Americans, asked for laws to prohibit blacks from entering certain occupations. When their legal efforts failed, they

A railroad conductor orders a free, well-dressed African American to leave a first-class car during the 1850s. Although such blatant racial discrimination was against some state laws, it was practiced widely, even in the "liberal" North.

sought to discourage blacks by refusing to take them on as apprentices. Frederick Douglass's call for an industrial school was one response to the economic limitations faced by African Americans. Even without the school, the number of skilled craftsmen among the free black population remained relatively stable, as former slave artisans willingly trained other blacks. Through hard work and perseverance, free blacks entered scores of occupations, including tailoring, paperhanging, cooking, construction, and shipbuilding. A small segment of the population became teachers, ministers, and physicians.

Harriet E. Wilson, a freeborn black who lived in Boston in the 1850s, found it almost impossible to earn enough money to support herself and her son. Believing she had a formula that prevented hair from graying, she tried making a living in the beauty trade, but poor health forced her to give up the business. Bedridden, she turned to writing. Wilson's somewhat autobiographical *Our Nig; or, Sketches from the Life of a Free Black* appeared in 1859, making Wilson the first African American woman to publish a novel in the United States. But despite the book's innovative style, the public virtually ignored it, and it failed to bring Wilson enough money to support herself.

Racial discrimination hit free blacks in public as well as in the workplace, but not all its victims accepted it peacefully. One evening in 1853, for example, Sarah Parker Remond, a freeborn black abolitionist, purchased a ticket for an opera performance at Boston's Howard Athenaeum. The theater manager not only refused to seat her but had her thrown out, injuring her in the process. Remond sued and won a hefty $500 judgment. In this case at least, the court recognized blatant racism and injustice.

Perhaps hearing of Remond's experience, a New York City woman instituted a lawsuit the following year. Ordered to sit in the back of a trolley car, Elizabeth Jennings sued the Third Avenue Railroad Company for practicing discrimination on public transportation. Declaring that "colored persons, if sober, well-behaved and free from disease" could travel in the New York City cars without segregated seating, the court awarded Jennings damages of $225.

Sometimes whites invited African American artists to perform but barred blacks from their audience. When Elizabeth Taylor Greenfield made her debut at New York's Metropolitan Hall in 1853, no African Americans witnessed the occasion. Frederick Douglass criticized the singer for performing under those conditions. "We marvel that Miss Greenfield can allow herself to be treated with such palpable disrespect," he wrote, "for the insult is to her, not less than to her race."

Douglass also criticized Lucy Stone, a white feminist and abolitionist who lectured at Philadelphia's Music Fund Hall under similar circumstances. Stone protested the policy during her speech, but for Douglass such gestures were not enough. "The course of duty was plain," he wrote in *Frederick Douglass's Paper*. By remaining in the hall, he argued, Stone lost an opportunity to deal a "blow for freedom, upon the hoary head of the monster prejudice." Douglass believed that Stone's walking away in protest would have impressed her audience far more than the speech she delivered.

Keenly aware of the obstacles that faced them, African Americans tried to work toward change. A Negro Convention Movement took shape, and its leaders organized local, state, and national meetings in an effort to provide black activists with a sense of direction. The conventions met in northern cities and used petitions and public addresses to seek civil and political rights.

Black leaders developed a wide variety of approaches to the oppression and discrimination faced by African Americans. In 1851 Negro Convention delegates proposed the formation of military companies. Several years later Kentucky-born William Wells Brown, who had escaped from slavery in 1834, urged free African Americans "to be united to a man, in opposition to the American union." Frederick Douglass opposed such radicalism, favoring instead the integration of African Americans into mainstream American society. The freeborn Martin Delany advocated emigration from the United States.

As they debated these alternatives, the conventioneers agreed to protest Ohio's Black Code—a set of laws discriminating against African Americans—and a New York law mandating that blacks had to

When leading suffragist and abolitionist Lucy Stone agreed to address an exclusively white Philadelphia audience, she angered Frederick Douglass, who said her appearance had done more harm than good.

Radical political activist William Wells Brown was also a radical author. His 1853 novel, Clotel; or, the President's Daughter, *not only damned slavery but created a scandal by suggesting that President Thomas Jefferson had sired a black child.*

prove they owned at least $250 worth of property before they could vote. The conventioners also followed national events, paying special attention to developments likely to affect African Americans.

While free blacks fought to improve their standing, the majority of African Americans remained in bondage. In 1850 approximately half of all enslaved people lived on plantations with at least 20 other bondservants. The remainder worked on small farms or as domestic servants or artisans in rural and urban areas. An estimated 5 percent of all slaves were skilled laborers. Boys became smiths, masons, and wheelwrights. Girls learned such domestic tasks as cooking, sewing, spinning, and weaving.

Most bondservants worked as fieldhands, cultivating such cash crops as cotton, rice, sugar, and tobacco. Men and women performed many of the same tasks: plowing, cultivating, and harvesting. While the women worked, they often left their younger children in the care of slaves who were either too young or too old to perform other chores. Women often took their babies along with them into the fields. They sometimes strapped the infants to their backs and sometimes left them resting on mats at the end of their rows, returning periodically to move them out of the sun or nurse them.

On larger plantations, youths, pregnant women, and older men and women often worked in "trash gangs." In these special units children learned to perform agricultural chores. Once in the workforce, children were subjected to the same punishments as adults. Almost all accounts of slavery mention whippings. Although there were certainly many slaves who never experienced corporal punishment, the practice was so pervasive that it caused apprehension among blacks throughout the South.

The massive workload imposed on most slaves limited the amount of time they could spend with

their families. After work, parents and children often gathered in their cabins to share meals and discuss family matters. Youngsters learned behavior that was appropriate for children and slaves from these family gatherings. The adage "Children are to be seen and not heard" had a special meaning in slave families, for it discouraged children from divulging family secrets to whites.

Enslaved families observed a division of labor in the slave quarters. Women attended to domestic chores with the help of young girls. Men, often accompanied by boys, hunted game and caught fish to increase their food supply. Slaves sometimes also supplemented their rations by cul-

Fieldhands—male, female, young, and old—make their weary way home after a long, hot day of picking cotton. The majority of American slaves worked on plantations or farms.

in 1854. In "The Slave Mother," Harper wrote,

They tear him from her circling arms
Her last and fond embrace:—
Oh! never more may her sad eyes
Gaze on his mournful face.

Poems on Miscellaneous Subjects sold more than 10,000 copies in three years. Three nationally distributed newspapers, including William Lloyd Garrison's *Liberator*, reprinted Harper's "Eliza Harris," a poem based on a character from *Uncle Tom's Cabin*. Harper's interest in women's rights, moral reform, and abolition made her one of the most popular writers of her time.

Many slaveholders considered themselves the benevolent guardians of their slaves, whom they assumed to be too naive to make decisions for themselves. What slaves thought of their owners was

An 1862 photograph shows Sunday on a South Carolina plantation: the men rest and the women perform domestic chores. In most enslaved families, women took care of the house, men brought game to the table, and the whole family worked in the fields.

probably another matter. Those who were able to write of their experiences often explained that before their owners they wore an expression that worked like a mask, hiding their true feelings. Former slave Henry Bibb admitted in his autobiography that "the only weapon of self defense that I could use successfully was that of deception." The maxim "Got one mind for the boss to see; got another for what I know is me" helped slaves perform public acts of deference to whites while maintaining their self-respect.

The number of bondservants who challenged their owners by running away or resisting their orders—working slowly or destroying crops or property—gives the lie to the notion that, as historian Eugene D. Genovese has put it, slaves and their owners melded "into one people with genuine elements of affection and intimacy." Even when the relationship between slave and slaveholder appeared harmonious, beneath the surface the slave's struggle for autonomy continued. That struggle did not end until slavery ceased to exist.

Sold to a new master, a boy is torn from his mother's arms in this book illustration from the 1850s. "The Slave Mother," Frances E. Harper's hugely popular poem, dealt with forced separation, one of slavery's most cruel features.

5

"I WROTE PASSES FOR MY GRANDMOTHER"

MY School Children that comes to school every day are improving in learning," wrote Lucy Skipwith, an Alabama slave, in an 1854 letter to her owner. The addressee, John Hartwell Cocke, had given Skipwith permission to open a school at Hopewell, his plantation in Green County, Alabama, several years earlier. Having emancipated many of Skipwith's relatives and sent them to Liberia in 1833, he was preparing to free the rest of the Hopewell slaves, and he hoped to encourage them to become more independent before they followed the first group to Africa. Cocke believed that education led to self-sufficiency, and in this conviction he had supported Skipwith's efforts to teach the Hopewell children.

After running the school for some time, Skipwith realized that her pupils would have difficulty learning if they did not attend classes every day. These children worked in the fields picking cotton along with their parents, and every year at harvesttime they were

A master teaches two slave children to read. Although most southern states outlawed literacy for slaves, some slaveholders, such as John Hartwell Cocke, made a sincere effort to educate their bondspeople.

59

Nat Turner, a literate Virginia slave born in 1800, holds a secret meeting to urge his fellow slaves to revolt. In the panic created by the bloody uprising that followed, some states toughened their laws against slave education.

forced to miss their lessons. On August 17, Skipwith wrote to Cocke in the hope that he would allow her pupils to miss work to attend school.

When Cocke refused, Skipwith set up a night school, and by May 1855 she was able to brag that the children were learning to write and could add, subtract, and multiply. Still, at cotton-picking time they continued to work from early morning until dark, and they were often too tired to attend classes afterward. Skipwith tried to make up for this loss by teaching the children regularly on Sunday, their day of rest.

The efforts of Lucy Skipwith, John Hartwell Cocke, and others like them made it possible for some slaves to move beyond the drudgery of day-to-day life and seek solace and inspiration in the written word. Although official records place the proportion of literate slaves in 1860 at 5 percent, many historians believe this estimate is too low. In a series of interviews conducted by the Works Progress Administration (WPA) in the 1930s, Sarah Fitzpatrick, who had worked as a house servant during the slave era, explained that slaves who could read and write often "kept that up their sleeve. . . . They played dumb like they couldn't read a bit."

Those who learned to read against their owners' wishes lived with the threat of punishment. Doc Daniel Dowdy told WPA interviewers, "The first time you was caught trying to read or write, you was whipped with a cow-hide, the next time with a cat-o-nine-tails and the third time they cut the first jint [joint] offen your forefinger." Such frightening stories discouraged some would-be scholars, and they encouraged secrecy and deceit among those who did become literate.

After 1831, when the literate slave Nat Turner led a major rebellion in Virginia, some slave states enacted laws against slave education. These laws were not always enforced, and some included provisions that allowed slaves to learn reading and writing under certain conditions. The state of Virginia, for example, permitted slaveholders to teach their slaves individually. These exceptions to the general rule made such projects as the Hopewell school possible.

Nonslaveholders who chose to teach slaves in Virginia and other states were subject to harsh punishment. Free African Americans were to receive 20 lashes; white offenders could be fined up to $50 and spend two months in prison. Salaried whites found guilty of instructing slaves

Plantation workers listen intently as their owner's daughter reads the Bible. Braving the harsh penalties for teaching blacks to read and write, many whites and free blacks quietly offered schooling to slaves.

could be fined up to $100 per offense depending upon the court. Still, many bold individuals violated the law. Mary Smith Peake, a free mulatto woman, started a school in Hampton, Virginia, in the early 1850s. Local authorities must have known about her school, for she ran it in her home, one block off the main thoroughfare, Queen Street. Yet apparently they chose to overlook the project; Peake taught enslaved and free pupils without interference for 10 years.

An untold number of slaves who could not attend school were educated informally by white women and children. Susie King Taylor, a Georgia slave, learned to read and write from a playmate. The children knew their actions would anger the white girl's father, and the two agreed to keep the lessons secret. The girl's mother was aware of their project but did not interfere.

Taylor later used her reading and writing skills to challenge the rules laid down by her owner. Slaves were not to leave their owner's property without written permission. "I often wrote passes for my grandmother," wrote Taylor. These tickets to the outside world "were good until 10 or 11:00 P.M. for one night or every night for one month."

It was power of this kind that made educated slaves a threat to slaveholders. If literate slaves were bold enough to grant themselves, or others, permission to travel for days or weeks at a time, many slaveholders wondered, what reason would they have to return when the pass expired? Slaveholders also feared that slaves who could learn more about the world beyond the homes, farms, or plantations where they worked were more likely to become restless. With some justification many slaveholders believed that if they kept their bondservants ignorant and isolated, they would remain easier to control.

For free African Americans living in the southern cities and northern states, education was somewhat easier to come by, although it involved financial burdens that not everyone could carry. Northern-born black abolitionist Maria W. Stewart organized a school for black children in Baltimore in 1852. Her basic curriculum included reading, writing, spelling, and arithmetic. The students paid 50 cents per month, an amount that barely allowed Stewart to maintain the school. Later she learned that other schools charged $1 a month for writing lessons alone.

In 1852 a white contemporary of Stewart, Myrtilla Miner, founded the Normal School for Colored Girls in Washington, D.C. So-called normal schools prepared students for the teaching profession. When

SCHOOL FOR COLORED GIRLS

A white mob attacks a black girls' school in Canterbury, Connecticut, in 1833. Fear of an educated black population was by no means limited to the South.

Miner had trouble finding a permanent location for the school, she had her own building constructed, using funds donated by Quakers in New York, Pennsylvania, and New England.

Once completed, the school was well equipped. It boasted a large library and facilities for teaching everything from history to horticulture. Students heard lectures on contemporary scientific and literary topics and learned to appreciate fine art by studying the school's collection of paintings and engravings.

Miner's ambition, she wrote, was to make the institute a "first-class teachers' college." To fulfill that dream, she went on fund-raising tours during the summer months, although it became more difficult for her to travel as her health failed. She did not live to see her dream become a reality, but the normal school continued to develop after her death and eventually became part of the University of the District of Columbia.

Sarah Mapps Douglass was another northern-born black dedicated to the education of African Americans. In 1853 she began teaching at the Institute for Colored Youth in Philadelphia, where she was responsible for the Girls' Department. Not content with the school's traditional reading, writing, arithmetic, geography, and spelling courses, she introduced such new subjects as physiology into the curriculum. Douglass enrolled in medical courses at the Ladies Institute of Pennsylvania Medical University in order to expand her teaching repertoire.

Some blacks attended colleges founded specifically for African Americans. Ashmun Institute, later known as Lincoln University, opened with Presbyterian sponsorship January 1, 1854. Situated in Oxford, Pennsylvania, Lincoln is now the oldest institution of higher education for African Americans in the United States. Ashmun admitted its first students two years after receiving its charter. In 1855 the Cincinnati Conference of the African Methodist Episcopal Church established another black college, Wilberforce University, named for an English abolitionist. Many of the school's earliest students were mulattoes who moved to Ohio after their white fathers emancipated them.

Free blacks could also attend some white-run institutions of higher learning. Fanny Jackson Coppin, who was to become principal of Philadelphia's Institute for Colored Youth, attended Rhode Island State Normal School. Medical schools at Boston's Harvard College and the University of New York admitted African Americans. Students interested in the ministry could study at theological seminaries in Gettysburg, Pennsylvania; Hanover, New Hampshire; and Charleston, South Carolina.

Horse-drawn vehicles roll across the campus of Ohio's Wilberforce University in this 1856 lithograph. Established by the African Methodist Episcopal Church in 1855, Wilberforce attracted many emancipated blacks and mulattoes.

Oberlin Collegiate Institute (now Oberlin College), near Elyria, Ohio, had enrolled nearly 100 African American men and women by 1865. Although blacks made up only about 4 percent of its student population, Oberlin, according to historian Carter G. Woodson, "did so much for the eduction of Negroes before the Civil War that it was often spoken of as an institution for the education of the people of color." Students could complete Oberlin's Greek and Latin admission requirements through study in public high schools, private schools, or in the college's preparatory department. John Russwurm, the first African American college graduate, and Frederick Douglass's daughters were among those who attended Oberlin.

Most of the women at Oberlin enrolled in what was known as the Young Ladies Course, which did not require Latin, Greek, or higher mathematics. Lucy Stanton, the program's first black female graduate, completed course requirements in 1850. Ten of the 16 African Americans who graduated from Oberlin in the following decade were women in the Young Ladies Course. Like Stanton, these women went on to become teachers.

In 1859 the daughter of a Chippewa Indian woman and an African American man entered Oberlin at the expense of her brother, a California gold miner. Known as Wildfire by her tribe, she changed her name at Oberlin to Mary Edmonia Lewis. After completing Oberlin's preparatory courses she entered the liberal arts program. A moderately successful student, she left without graduating, then moved to Boston, where, using letters of introduction from Oberlin, she met William Lloyd Garrison and Edward Brackett, a well-known artist with whom Garrison was acquainted. Lewis, who aspired "to make the form of things," eventually become the first major female sculptor of African American heritage.

Many black students could not afford to pay the full cost of a college course, and it was not uncommon for schools to allow them to earn their tuition by doing manual labor. Because their participants performed much-needed services, these programs generally benefited the school as much as the students.

With the help of dedicated teachers, philanthropists, and liberal institutions, a significant number of 19th-century African Americans learned to read, write, and study a variety of academic subjects. Many of them had to travel far from home to attend school, and they used their newly won knowledge to preserve family ties through letters. Those who graduated from schools of higher learning often went on to work as community leaders, teachers, ministers, and reformers, taking their own turn at improving the lives of fellow African Americans.

6

THE STORM,
THE WHIRLWIND, AND
THE EARTHQUAKE

ABOLITIONISTS engaged in both public and private acts of protest. They assaulted slavery through the press, from the pulpit, and on the lecture circuit. They wrote letters to antislavery journals and spoke against bondage in churches and other public places. Some participated in open demonstrations against the recapture of fugitives; others secretly assisted runaways. The form of protest mattered little, as long as it led to their objective: the freedom of the enslaved.

By the mid-19th century, antislavery activists had come to an agreement on what had long been a major point of contention: the timing of emancipation. Some opponents of slavery believed that the institution would disappear in time, and that to rush its demise would be unwise. Another faction believed that, as historian Benjamin Quarles puts it, the "gradualist" approach was "wrong in theory, weak in practice, and fatally quieting to the conscience of the

Flanked by a trunkful of antislavery literature, a New England abolitionist awaits the stagecoach to her next lecture stop. In the decade before the Civil War, such crusaders crisscrossed the country, speaking in any hall available to them.

69

Silver-tongued and elegant, the freeborn abolitionist Charles Lenox Remond was immensely popular on the lecture circuit. The Massachusetts native often appeared with his sister Sarah Parker Remond, herself a spellbinding orator on slavery.

slaveholder." It was this group that dominated the antislavery movement in the 1850s.

Even among the so-called immediatists, however, the movement was divided, for most participants made a distinction between antislavery supporters and abolitionists. The antislavery factions were more reticent than the abolitionists, who became known as the most radical opponents of slavery. The rhetoric used by abolitionists, which included such language as "man-thief," "child-seller," and "willful liar," helped mark them as uncompromising reformers.

By the 1850s, former slaves were adding a third element to the antislavery movement. Addressing large crowds on the abolitionist lecture circuit, freed men and women gave their own accounts of slavery's horrors. In the early part of the decade, the freeborn Charles Lenox Remond was the movement's best-known African American abolitionist. He and his sister Sarah Parker Remond often traveled together to speak on behalf of bondservants. Later Henry Bibb, William Wells Brown, and Frederick Douglass became known as the most talented black lecturers. Sojourner Truth appeared on the abolitionist platform, but she was never the featured speaker. Program organizers knew that she would deliver a short, entertaining, and somewhat idiosyncratic speech. Douglass, on the other hand, balanced his eloquent speeches with flashes of passionate anger and prudent wisdom, making him the star of the abolitionist stage.

Douglass used the abolitionist platform to expose the gulf between rhetoric and reality in American democracy. He spoke against "America's ideological pretensions" and argued that the slave's fight for freedom was comparable to the battle waged by the leaders of the American Revolution. On July 4, 1852, in Rochester, New York, Douglass gave a speech examining the meaning of liberty and democracy. Entitling his address "What to the Slave Is the Fourth of July," Douglass told his audience, "I am not included within the pale of this glorious anniversary." African Americans, he pointed out, did not enjoy the justice and liberty guaranteed by the Declaration of Independence. "You may rejoice," Douglass declared; "I must mourn." He continued:

Standing with God and the crushed and bleeding slave on this occasion, I will, in the name of humanity which is outraged, in the name of liberty which is fettered, in the name of the Constitution and the Bible, which are disregarded and trampled upon, dare to call in question and to denounce, with all the emphasis I can command, everything that serves to perpetuate slavery—the great sin and shame of America!

Douglass was a powerful speaker who did not mince words. He believed that only the "storm, the whirlwind, and the earthquake" would rouse the nation to abolish slavery.

Struck by Douglass's elevated rhetoric, white abolitionists sometimes worried that his listeners would doubt that he was a former slave. When advised to tell his story with "a little of the plantation speech," and not appear "too learned," Douglass refused. He would tolerate control by abolitionists no more than he had the beatings of the "slavebreaker" who had unsuccessfully tried to tame him during his days in bondage.

Of the free black women who lectured on the abolitionist circuit in the 1850s, Frances Harper was among the most successful. She accepted a position as a traveling lecturer for the Maine Anti-Slavery Society in 1854, delivering 33 lectures in 21 widely separated towns in less than two months. William Wells Brown called Harper's arguments "forcible, her appeals pathetic, her logic fervent, her imagination fervid, and her delivery original and easy." She spoke often to African American audiences.

As well as making speeches, freed blacks wrote autobiographical narratives that functioned as abolitionist propaganda. Abolitionist newspapers occasionally serialized or reprinted the life stories of former slaves. Many blacks also published their narratives in book form, either independently or with the help of their educated supporters.

The era's best-known slave narrative is Frederick Douglass's *My Bondage and My Freedom* (1855), the second of three autobiographies written by the multitalented former slave. An enlarged edition of *Narrative of the Life of Frederick Douglass, My Bondage (1845)* portrays slavery's impact on the writer at various stages in his life. Douglass's language in this volume is characteristically aggressive and compelling.

Harper, a regular contributor to abolitionist newspapers, employed poetry to protest slavery. Her poem "A Mother's Heroism" commemorates Elijah P. Lovejoy, a white abolitionist murdered by a mob in Alton, Illinois, in 1837. The work centers on Lovejoy's mother, who supported his beliefs. Rather than eliciting pity for the bereaved woman, Harper seeks sympathy for the abolitionist cause.

> The main audience for antislavery literature was the northern reading public, for slaveowners generally blocked its distribution in the South. This does not mean that black southerners, free or enslaved, remained uninformed about the activities of antislavery activists. Household bondservants overheard conversations about the movement as they worked, and slaves living in towns often enjoyed some contact with free blacks, who could share their information.

Meanwhile, it was in such northern and midwestern cities as New York, Boston, Philadelphia, Cleveland, and Detroit that abolitionists carried out their main campaign. Aside from educating the public about the cruelties of bondage, they organized committees that provided assistance to fugitive slaves. The Detroit Vigilance Committee, for example, helped more than 1,000 fugitives in the 1850s. The Fugitive Aid Society in Syracuse, New York, helped fugitive slaves secure freedom and find employment. Jermain W. Loguen, the manager of the society, aided his

Entitled A Bold Stroke for Freedom, *this lithograph appeared in a contemporary book on the Underground Railroad. Northerners thrilled to tales of blacks overcoming desperate odds to gain their liberty.*

charges by urging local residents to hire them.

Antislavery committees also provided fugitives with food and other necessities. Proceeds from fairs and concerts, as well as gifts donated by church congregations, helped defray the committees' expenses. Women's auxiliaries and charitable organizations in England also contributed to their cause. And in 1859 Loguen unexpectedly received a cash donation from 30 escaped slaves he had helped.

Despite the generosity of its supporters, the abolitionist movement, like other philanthropic endeavors, was hampered by a constant shortage of resources. The fund-raiser's task was made more difficult by the general poverty imposed on blacks by discrimination in employment. To make matters worse, individuals sometimes posed as antislavery activists in order to make their own profits, either as swindlers or as paid informers. In 1858 an informer named John Brodie discovered that betrayers of the abolitionist cause could pay dearly for their actions. When a group of black abolitionists in Cincinnati, Ohio, heard that Brodie had received $300 for exposing fugitives, they seized him and threatened to strike a blow for each dollar he had received. The black abolitionist leader Henry Highland Garnet stopped the whipping, and Brodie placed himself in the local jail for safekeeping.

Fugitives fleeing their owners needed support not only in the North but all along the route from their place of bondage to their ultimate destination. Those who were lucky found such help in the abolitionist network known as the Underground Railroad. Most fugitives, however, received assistance only after they had avoided capture and reached the North.

Escaping from bondage often involved heartrending decisions about leaving family and friends behind. Still, it was not unusual for parents to encourage their children to run away alone. In his autobiography, William Wells Brown wrote that his mother and sister insisted that he escape without them. "If we cannot get our liberty," said Brown's sister, "we do not wish to be the means of keeping you from a land of freedom." Devout Christians, she and her mother believed that all of them would eventually meet in heaven.

The best-organized section of the Underground Railroad was a stretch manned by Joseph C. Bustill, Elijah F. Pennypacker, and William Still. The New Jersey–born Still served as an operator in southeastern Pennsylvania between 1849 and 1861. His interest in fugitive slaves was connected to his own family history. From early childhood Still knew that when his mother had escaped from slavery, she had been forced to leave two of his brothers behind. Eventually, one brother escaped and found his way to the Underground Railroad station in Philadelphia. Still, who

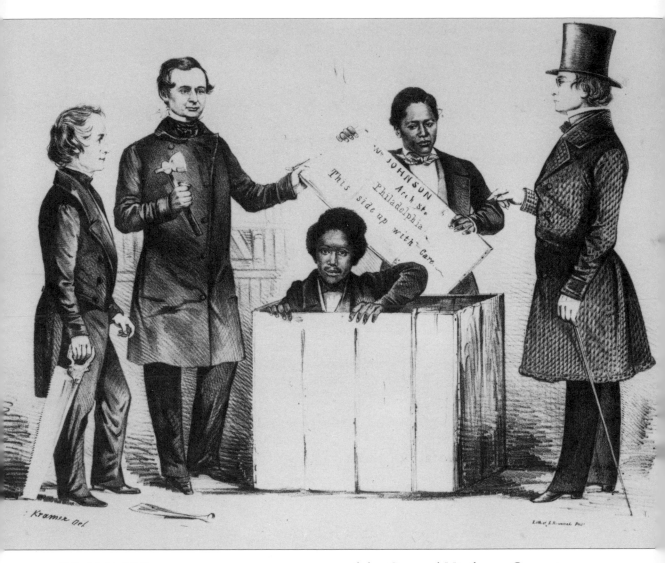

Philadelphia Vigilance Committee officials unpack Henry "Box" Brown, a Virginian who escaped slavery via a wooden crate. Holding the lid is William Still, an outstanding "station master" of the Underground Railroad.

was secretary of the General Vigilance Committee at the time, learned of his brother's identity while collecting information about the runaways.

One of the earliest and most fascinating accounts of a successful escape from slavery is the story of Henry "Box" Brown of Richmond, Virginia. After praying for "aid in bursting [slavery's] fetters asunder," Brown decided to attempt a unique means of escape. "I was willing to dare even death itself rather than endure any longer the clanking of those galling chains," wrote Brown in his autobiography. Having resolved to flee, Brown asked a white friend to build a crate measuring three feet wide and two and one-half feet high, and to seal him into it. With the help of other friends, he arranged to have himself shipped 350 miles from Richmond to the Philadelphia Vigilance Committee office. He took a small quantity of water, and breathed through three small holes drilled in the crate.

The rough handling of the box, the cramped space, and fear of detection tested Brown's will severely. "The sufferings I had thus to endure seemed like an age to me," Brown recalled, "but I resolved to conquer or die." The flight to freedom ended in Philadelphia among new friends. Brown climbed out of the box as a man "risen . . . from the dead," just one of the estimated 5,000 runaways who passed through Philadelphia in the 1850s.

Maryland-born Harriet Tubman, who fled from slavery in 1849, was unusual on two accounts. First, although women of childbearing age were less likely than men to run away from slavery, Tubman ran away while her husband remained behind. Second, Tubman would not rest content until she had brought her family out of bondage; after she had reached safety, she repeatedly returned to the South to rescue others, including her parents and siblings.

While living in Philadelphia, Tubman developed a close working relationship with William Still, and eventually became one of the Underground Railroad's most celebrated conductors. Tubman is credited with at least 19 trips to the South to rescue more than 300 enslaved men, women, and children. Unable to read or write, she succeeded through unwavering courage, quick wits, amazing resourcefulness, and a lack of tolerance for fugitives who changed their minds. Tubman carried a gun to keep the fainthearted from turning back and exposing her plans; she encouraged

Harriet Tubman, who escaped from slavery in 1849, prepares to address an abolition meeting in the 1850s. Small, sickly, yet tough as iron, Tubman repeatedly risked her life by returning to the South to rescue more than 300 other slaves.

many a faltering passenger with the words, "Move or die!"

Abolitionists who lived along the route Tubman traveled soon came to know her, and they assisted her whenever possible. Thomas Garrett, a Wilmington, Delaware, resident, hid runaways in his shoe store. Some associates also helped Tubman financially, although for the most part she supported her project by working as a cook and a maid. Sometimes she guided passengers all the way to Canada in order to place them beyond the grasp of slave catchers.

Underground Railroad agents such as Harriet Tubman challenged slavery directly. Other abolitionists used the public forum to win supporters of their cause. In 1854 these two campaigns combined with a turn of political events to catapult slavery into the center of national politics. Until the slavery issue was resolved, tensions would continue to run high throughout the nation.

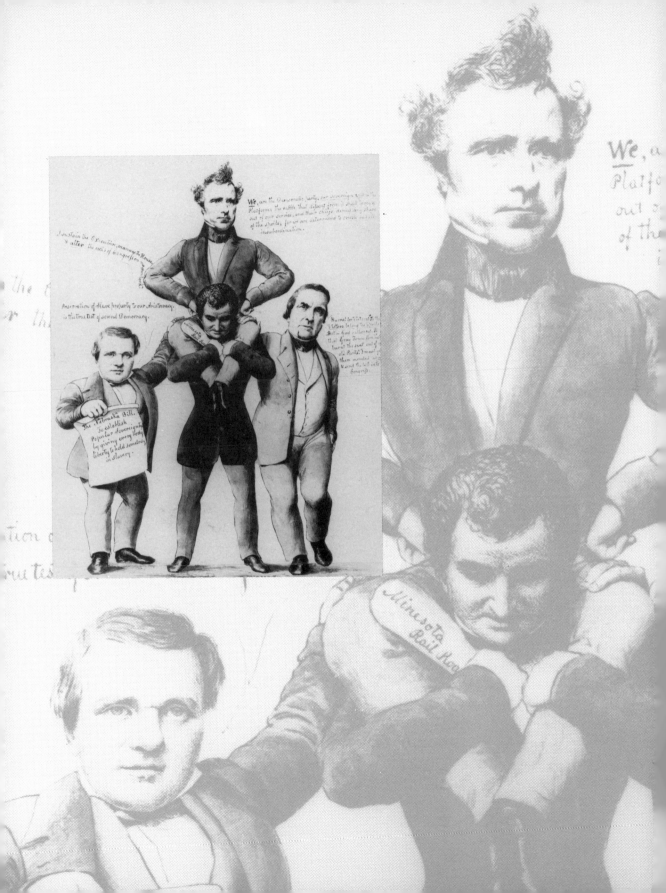

7

THE LEGACY OF ANTHONY BURNS

THE slaves guided by Harriet Tubman found freedom, but many who fled on their own met disaster. Among these doomed beings were Margaret Garner and her family, Kentucky runaways whose pursuers caught up with them in Ohio in 1856. Cornered by the slave catchers and maddened by the thought of returning to bondage, Garner brought out a concealed butcher knife and slashed the throat of her little daughter. When she was brought to court, she asked to be executed. "I would go singing to the gallows," she told the judge, "rather than be returned to slavery." Rejecting her plea, he returned Garner to her master. Novelist Toni Morrison based her 1984 Pulitzer Prize–winning novel, *Beloved*, on Garner's tragic story.

Whether they succeeded or not, few escape attempts received widespread attention, for throughout most of the 1850s they were overshadowed by other issues. One of these was the Kansas-Nebraska Bill,

Deriding the 1854 Kansas-Nebraska Bill—which let the voters of those states decide the slavery question—this cartoon shows President Franklin Pierce astride Congress. Bill sponsor Stephen Douglas (left) holds a paper reading: "The Nebraska Bill. To establish popular sovereignty by giving everybody liberty to hold somebody in slavery."

proposed federal legislation that would allow the settlers of Kansas and Nebraska to decide on the slavery
question for themselves.

President Franklin Pierce had been in the White
House less than a year when Senator Stephen A.
Douglas of Illinois, chairman of the Committee on
Territories, introduced the Kansas-Nebraska Bill in
1854. At this point, Congress was debating the merits
of a transcontinental railroad that would link the
well-settled Atlantic Coast with the developing Pa-
cific Coast. At the heart of the national debate was
the railroad's route; whatever city housed the road's
eastern terminus—the point where trains from the
West would meet and exchange cargo and passengers
with trains from the East—stood to profit hugely.
Representatives of various states, therefore, vied des-
perately to have the road's terminus in their area.

In order to improve the chances of a northern
route—which would terminate at Douglas's choice,
Chicago—Douglas wanted to bring order to the un-
settled, unorganized Indian country of Nebraska and
Kansas. His Kansas-Nebraska Bill would do just that.
And in order to make the bill acceptable to the South,
it included the "popular sovereignty" section, which
left the slavery issue up to the settlers. The senator
claimed that he did not care one way or the other
about slavery—the main issue addressed by the bill—
but only wanted to see the West developed. He also
hoped the project would help him win the Democratic
presidential nomination.

> **Douglas's bill essentially negated the 1820
> Missouri Compromise, which prohibited slavery
> in the 1803 Louisiana Purchase territory north
> of 36° 30". Antislavery congressmen called the
> Kansas-Nebraska Bill a base violation of a 30-
> year-old pledge against extending slavery in the
> region, but after a three-month debate Congress**

passed it, and in May 1854 President Pierce signed it into law. Because it overturned the Missouri Compromise, the Kansas-Nebraska Act outraged the North, which directed its fury against Douglas. Perceived as a cat's-paw for the slaveholding South, he lost his last chance to win the presidency.

And because northerners saw the Kansas-Nebraska Act as a tool with which the South intended to push slavery into the western territories, they gradually pulled away from existing political parties and formed a new one: the Republican party, the voice of the abolitionists. The Republicans showed their strength in the 1854 elections, electing a majority in the House of Representatives and gaining control of a number of northern state governments. The Kansas-Nebraska Act thus set in motion the wheels that would drive the nation toward civil war.

Frederick Douglass, infuriated by the act and its potential consequences, reacted strongly. "Slavery, like rape, robbery, piracy or murder, has no right to exist in any part of the world," he roared. "Neither north or south of 36 deg. 30 min. shall it have a moment's repose, if I can help it." The former slave continued bitter denunciations of the bill in his newspaper and public lectures. Douglass also wrote to politicians and private citizens urging them to support better legislation.

The passage of the Kansas-Nebraska Act coincided with the most dramatic and controversial of all reactions to the Fugitive Slave Act of 1850. In February 1854 Virginia-born slave Anthony Burns escaped from his owner, Charles Suttle, and fled to Boston. Suttle learned of Burns's whereabouts from a letter the

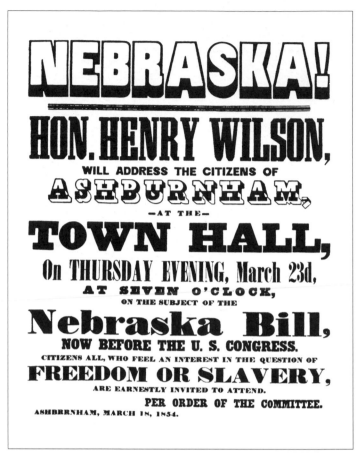

An 1854 handbill summons all Nebraskans to a lecture on the Kansas-Nebraska Bill, then under debate in the U.S. Senate. Not only midwesterners but most Americans held passionate views on the bill's effect on slavery.

fugitive wrote to his brother, who remained in bondage at the Suttle home. In May, Suttle went to Boston to retrieve the runaway, who had been arrested and jailed on a bogus robbery charge.

In 1854, Boston was one of the nation's main bastions of abolitionism. Home of William Lloyd Garrison's *Liberator* and the American Anti-Slavery Society, the Massachusetts city was described by one southern U.S. senator as "the theater upon which agitators, whether natives or foreigners, carry on their operations against the domestic peace and quiet of the country." As soon as Boston activists learned of Burns's arrest, they resolved to help him defy both his owner and the Fugitive Slave Act of 1850.

This was not the first serious conflict between Boston abolitionists and the law. In 1851, some 30 black Bostonians had helped Frederick "Shadrach" Wilkins, a Virginia-born fugitive, evade his owner; rushing the courthouse where he was held, they freed him, then helped him flee to Canada. Later that year, another Boston group failed in its attempt to thwart the Fugitive Slave Act by helping the runaway Thomas Sims from Georgia. Unfortunately for the antislavery faction, these early acts of defiance had only made the federal government more adamant about returning runaways to slavery.

Following Burns's arrest, African American lawyer Robert Morris and two white attorneys, Richard Dana and Charles M. Ellis, offered the fugitive their services. Burns accepted, and the group began legal proceedings immediately. Other acts of support followed. A group of Bostonians scheduled a rally at which a throng gathered to hear activists relate the Burns case to the Kansas-Nebraska Act. Emotions ran high. One

A mid-1850s map shows the battle lines drawn for the Kansas-Nebraska Bill. The slave states, which favored the bill, are darkly shaded; the free states, which opposed it, are white; the gray areas are territories still without a vote.

speaker reminded listeners of the revolutionary spirit that had once made Boston a center of political protest. (Before the Revolutionary War, Bostonians' radical defiance of British laws had led to the notorious Boston Massacre and the Boston Tea Party.) Then a speaker suggested meeting at the courthouse the next morning to take action against Burns's arrest. Someone else shouted, "Let's go tonight!"

A mass of protesters rushed to the courthouse where Burns was held. One group of men, most of them African Americans, used a battering ram to break the door open. Several tried to enter the building, but deputies stopped them. After a brief skirmish in which one deputy was killed, the crowd retreated. A second assault on the courthouse through a basement door also failed. A short time later, the city police and two artillery companies arrived, arresting several of the protesters and dispersing the crowd. The next morning the court ruled that Suttle indeed owned Burns and was entitled to return him to slavery. Burns's counselors asked for additional time, and the commissioner recessed the hearing until Monday, May 29, 1854.

Meanwhile, Leonard Grimes, pastor of the church that Burns attended, was raising money to purchase his freedom. In a short time, he and his friends had obtained pledges for $1,200, which Suttle accepted as a fair price for the slave. The only obstacle to the transaction was Benjamin F. Hallett, a federal district attorney determined to show the South that the government would faithfully abide by the Fugitive Slave Act. Hallett used one delaying tactic after another to block the sale that Saturday. Then he hinted that if Suttle dropped charges, the federal government might not pay for the expenses he had incurred in the case. More than 100 federal troops had been called out to guard the courthouse. The cost of this force, said Hallett, would no doubt fall on Suttle. Hallett's scheme worked; Suttle backed out of the sale.

The atmosphere was tense when the hearing began on the following Monday. Some 1,000 people had been milling around the courthouse on Saturday. By Monday the crowd had grown to 7,000, of whom some 1,000 were African Americans. The hearing continued for several days. Finally, on June 2, 1854, the court commissioner ruled that Burns was Suttle's runaway slave, and that he was legally obligated to return to slavery. The decision was a triumph for the South and a harsh blow to Burns and his supporters.

Burns's departure created one of the greatest spectacles of the 19th century. According to historians William and Jane Pease, on the day of Burns's return to slavery, Boston buildings were draped in black. A massive entourage escorted Burns to the harbor, where he was to board a ship to Virginia. The historians described the scene:

> Leading the procession was a detachment from the National Boston Lancers. After them came a company of United States infantry. They were followed by a company of marines. Next came Burns, inside a hollow square composed of sixty volunteer guards and flanked by another company of marines. At the rear followed a six-pound cannon, loaded and ready for use, and a final company of marines.

The military carried out its mission without any major confrontations.

The chartered steamer waited for Burns at the wharf. From this ship Burns was to be transferred to a revenue cutter in the harbor. There Burns was to join his owner for the final leg of his journey to Virginia and a life of bondage. The total cost of returning Anthony Burns to slavery, paid by the federal government, was about $50,000. The two-week drama centered on Anthony Burns illustrated the strain under which the nation labored. Angry northerners responded by passing personal-liberty laws that required the government to provide alleged runaways with

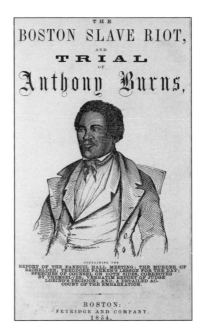

An 1854 book bearing a portrait of Anthony Burns contains a report on the fugitive slave and his attempted rescue, trial, and forcible return to slavery under the Fugitive Slave Act of 1850. The Burns case made headlines across the nation.

legal defense. The laws also prohibited the use of local and state facilities to detain blacks accused of leaving their owners.

As Burns returned to Virginia, a virtual civil war was developing in Kansas. In the March 1855 territorial election, thousands of proslavery agitators from nearby Missouri crossed the border and voted with the majority for slavery. The Kansas legislature legalized slavery and enacted the so-called Lecompton Constitution, which declared that "The right of property is before and higher than any constitutional sanction and the right of the owner of a slave . . . is the same and inalienable as the right of the owner of any property whatever."

By late summer 1855, large numbers of free-soil (antislavery) settlers had moved into the territory, denounced the proslavery government as fraudulent, and called a new convention in which they set up their own government. Historian James M. McPherson described the situation: "Kansas now had two territorial governments—one legal but fraudulent, the other illegal but representing a majority of settlers." The troubled territory would soon be known as "Bleeding Kansas."

One of the instigators of the Kansas upheaval was John Brown, a militant abolitionist from Connecticut. In 1855 Brown and several of his 20 children moved to Osawatomie, Kansas, to fight expansion of slavery in the territory. In May 1856 a proslavery posse entered the capital at Lawrence and set out to arrest the governing free-soilers. Riding with banners proclaiming SOUTHERN RIGHTS and LET YANKEES TREMBLE AND ABOLITIONISTS FALL, the posse destroyed the *Herald of Freedom* printing press, burned the Free State Hotel and the governor's house, and terrorized the town's residents. Five antislavery men died in the violence.

Brown, who considered himself God's instrument

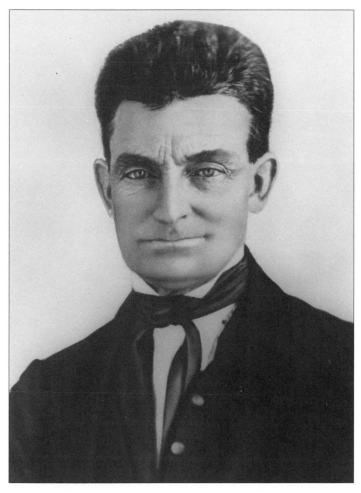

Fiery abolitionist John Brown retaliated for the 1856 murder of five antislavery Kansans by killing five proslavery settlers. The two acts sparked a bloody local war in which 200 more people died.

of revenge, responded to the attack by leading a small group of men to Pottawatomie Creek near Lawrence and killing five proslavery settlers. Within days, much of southeast Kansas was up in arms. In the fighting that followed, more than 200 people, including one of Brown's sons, were killed. Property losses were valued at nearly $2 million.

The tensions created by the Kansas-Nebraska Act manifested themselves at the local, state, and national levels. In 1856, after Massachusetts senator Charles Sumner fiercely denounced a South Carolina colleague who championed slavery, the man's nephew

"Southern Chivalry," an 1856 cartoon, shows South Carolina congressman Preston Brooks beating Massachusetts senator Charles Sumner on the Senate floor. Sumner's hostile remarks on the South and slavery triggered the attack.

attacked and severely injured Sumner with a heavy cane. Northerners saw the incident as an attack on free speech. It indicated the violent lengths to which the South would go in order to defend slavery.

The Kansas-Nebraska debate rekindled Kentucky-born Abraham Lincoln's interest in politics. Lincoln had served a single term as an Illinois representative in the U.S. Congress (1847–49) before returning to his legal practice. Commenting on the Kansas-Nebraska Bill, he protested that rather than encouraging liberty, it put slavery "on the high road to extension and perpetuity." Lincoln was not an abolitionist at the time, but he did favor gradual emancipation.

As the 1856 election drew near, the Republicans met in Pittsburgh and developed a platform that was critical of slavery as well as the Kansas-Nebraska Act. The party opposed the extension of slavery into the territories, although it raised no objections to states that excluded free African Americans. The Republicans nominated John C. Frémont, a celebrated explorer and former U.S. senator, for the presidency. The Democrats chose James Buchanan, who pledged not to interfere with slavery in the territories. The southern vote handed Buchanan the presidency.

At his inauguration, President Buchanan mentioned a forthcoming decision from the Supreme Court. He referred to the *Scott v. Sanford* (1857) case, which had become involved in national politics. The celebrated case involved a Missouri slave, Dred Scott, whose master, an army surgeon, had taken him to the free state of Illinois and to Minnesota Territory, where slavery was forbidden by the Missouri Compromise. The two finally returned to Missouri, where the doctor died.

At this point, local abolitionists persuaded Scott to sue for his freedom on the grounds that his residence in free territory had made him a free man. The action was to be a test case—one that seeks to clarify the law, in this case, whether slaves freed by living in a free state could have their freedom retracted.

The Missouri Supreme Court decided against Scott, but his lawyers appealed. Because the estate of Scott's deceased owner was handled by a relative from New York, John F. A. Sanford, Scott's lawyers decided to take the case to a federal court (where interstate matters are handled). It eventually went to the U.S. Supreme Court, to be argued in 1856.

According to the 54-page opinion by Chief Justice Roger B. Taney, Scott was not a U.S. citizen and could not, therefore, bring a lawsuit. Neither did living in a free territory emancipate him, said the Virginia-born Taney, because the Missouri Compromise was unconstitutional. It violated the Fifth Amendment, which protected property, including human chattel. Slaveholders, he said, could take their human property

Missouri slave Dred Scott became the center of an epic Supreme Court case when he sued for his freedom after his master took him to live in a free state. He lost: the court ruled that he was property and therefore without civil rights.

anywhere in the country, including the territories, without losing it.

What had begun as an uncomplicated suit developed into one of the most controversial legal cases in the history of the U.S. Supreme Court. Historian Walter Ehrlich wrote of the case, "The Court had sought to solve the volatile slavery issue; instead, what it did has been recorded as the most ill-advised and unfortunate moment in its history."

For the slaveholding South, the *Scott* decision was a great victory. Northerners, of course, reacted to it with alarm. Responding to it in a May 1857 speech to the American Anti-Slavery Society, Frederick Douglass called it a "demoniacal" judgment that blocked the way for equal rights and justice for all African Americans. "How deep is the misfortune of my poor, bleeding people, if this be so," he said sorrowfully. Generally optimistic even in the worst of times, Douglass continued:

> I have no fear that the National Conscience will be put to sleep by such an open, glaring, and scandalous tissue of lies as that decision is, and has been, over and over, shown to be. Such a decision cannot stand.

The political consequences of the Supreme Court decision overshadowed its personal impact on Scott. He had technically remained a slave during all the court proceedings, but he had been allowed to live as a free man, working at a variety of odd jobs in St. Louis, Missouri. After the Supreme Court decision, his "owner" legally emancipated him (and his family), and he became a St. Louis hotel porter. Scott had little time to savor his official freedom; in early 1858, he died of tuberculosis. His fate, however, was all but eclipsed amid the grave political tensions that it generated.

Thomas Jefferson had said the "momentous question" of slavery and its extension had "like a firebell in the night awakened and filled me with terror." The Scott decision hit the nation with the same force. "This very attempt to blot out forever the hopes of an enslaved people" only served, said Frederick Douglass, to "increase, intensify and embolden" their passion for freedom. Seemingly asleep for decades, the national conscience had now awakened with a jolt.

8

"WE MUST NOT BE ENEMIES"

ON June 16, 1858, Abraham Lincoln, having accepted the Republican Party's nomination for the U.S. Senate, opened his campaign with a powerful speech. Opposing the Kansas-Nebraska Act and the Democrat who introduced it, Stephen A. Douglas, Lincoln told his audience:

> A house divided against itself cannot stand. I believe this government cannot endure permanently half slave and half free. I do not expect the Union to be dissolved; I do not expect the house to fall; but I do expect it will cease to be divided. It will become all one thing, or all the other.

After this bold beginning, Lincoln challenged Douglas to seven debates. In the most memorable of these, held at Freeport, Illinois, Lincoln asked Douglas if there was any lawful way for the residents of a territory to exclude slavery before admission to statehood. Lincoln believed the *Dred Scott* decision had "rendered popular sovereignty as thin as soup boiled from the shadow of a pigeon that had starved to

Republican senatorial candidate Abraham Lincoln (standing), debates slavery with Democratic senator Stephen Douglas (at Lincoln's right) in 1858. One of seven verbal duels between the two men, this one took place in Freeport, Illinois.

95

Just over five feet tall but a mighty warrior on the speaker's platform, Stephen Douglas was widely known as "the little giant." This portrait, taken by famed Civil War photographer Mathew Brady, suggests the intellectual power of Lincoln's formidable adversary.

death." Douglas's reply, which became known as the "Freeport Doctrine," claimed that slavery could exist only where local regulations supported it. Lincoln lost the election, but he received national recognition for his position on slavery.

Meanwhile, John Brown was making plans to strike another blow at slavery, this time receiving financial support from the "Secret Six," a group of white abolitionists. African American abolitionists learned of Brown's plans for an armed rebellion as early as 1858. Brown received money from Mary Ellen Pleasant, a southern-born black who wanted the epitaph, "She was a Friend of John Brown's" on her grave marker. A Vigilance Committee member, Pleasant lived in Canada. She had met Brown when he visited Canada to attend the Provisional Constitution Convention and explain his venture to a party of black abolitionists.

Because Brown had a price on his head after the 1856 Pottawatomie Creek massacre, he tried to remain inconspicuous. Thus, one hot afternoon in August 1859, when he set up a meeting with Frederick Douglass in Chambersburg, Pennsylvania, it was at an abandoned quarry. Here, Brown told Douglass that he planned to raid the federal arsenal at Harpers Ferry, Virginia, some 50 miles distant. Once his men were armed, he said, they would move into the Appalachian mountains and head south to liberate slaves. Brown hoped for a general uprising throughout the South. He invited Douglass to join him.

The following day, the two men returned to the quarry and continued their discussion. Douglass was hesitant. Such a strike at the federal government would bring undue pressure upon the abolitionist movement. Douglass's arguments made no impression on Brown. "When my bees swarm," he said, "I'll need you to help hive them." Brown was referring to the millions of slaves who he assumed would readily join in the uprising.

Douglass could neither accept Brown's invitation nor convince him of the plan's futility. When Douglass advised him that death was the punishment for this treasonous activity, Brown is said to have responded, "Sometimes a man is worth more dead." But when Brown invited Harriet Tubman to join him she eagerly agreed, although an illness and a miscommunication prevented her from participating in the raid. Brown had ardent supporters among the African

Brown's five-day trial, which began October 27, 1859, generated enormous publicity. The defendant was literally unable to stand trial: suffering from a wound inflicted during his arrest, he lay on a cot throughout the proceedings. His lawyer tried to argue that Brown was insane, but the defendant showed no interest in supporting this argument. George Templeton Strong, a prominent New York Democrat, wrote about the trial: "The rigor of this Virginia court is right, but eminently inexpedient," he said. "The court should give Brown the maximum of indulgence and vigilantly shut out his prospective claim to the honors of martyrdom." After only 45 minutes of deliberation, however, the jury found Brown guilty.

On November 2, 1859, the convicted man returned to court for sentencing. In an eloquent five-minute speech he denied any intent to use violence and to "excite slaves to rebel, or make any general insurrection." The evidence clearly contradicted his testimony. When the death sentence was delivered, he responded, "I submit; so let it be done!"

In the month between the sentencing and his execution, Brown received visitors in his cell and continued to correspond with friends, family, and admirers. On November 25, 1859, Frances Harper wrote him a letter. Addressing Brown as "Dear Friend," she thanked him for extending his hand "to the crushed and blighted of my race." Harper hoped that "great good may arise to the cause of freedom" from Brown's "sad fate."

On December 2, 1859, when the time came for Brown to go to the gallows, he calmly climbed into a wagon and took a seat upon his own coffin. He carried a handwritten message that read:

> I John Brown am now quite certain that the crimes of this guilty land will never be purged away; but with Blood. I had as I now think vainly flattered myself that without very much bloodshed, it might be done.

Brown's execution was a national public event. More than 1,000 federal troops and members of the Virginia militia stood among a large crowd of spectators.

Although Frederick Douglass had taken no part in Brown's plan, before the trial started he fled to Canada briefly to avoid arrest. Meanwhile, despite the risk in doing so, Douglass defended Brown. The rebel was often portrayed as a business failure and religious zealot. At worst, he was seen as a madman. Douglass took exception to journals who cast him as "insane," claiming this was an attempt to divert attention from "Virginia's cowardly vengeance," Brown's execution. Douglass argued that Brown's conduct was "perfectly natural and simple on its face."

The dawn of a new decade brought no promises of peace. By the time of the 1860 presidential election, the Democratic party had split into a northern and southern wing. The northerners nominated Stephen Douglas, the southerners Kentuckian John C. Breckinridge, who had served as vice president under President Buchanan.

The Republicans met in Chicago and nominated Abraham Lincoln for president and Hannibal Hamlin, former governor of Maine and U.S. senator, as his running mate. The party expanded its platform to include issues related to the national economy. Lincoln won, but with only 40 percent of the popular vote. Because his name did not appear on ballots in the Deep South, he received no votes there.

At the time of the 1860 election, the slave population stood at 3,952,760. To be sure, abolitionists and others continued to help fugitives escape from bondage. A December 30, 1860, letter written by Martha C. Wright noted that seven fugitives had been "pioneered safely from

Abraham Lincoln was elected president of the United States in 1860. By the end of 1861, the 11 southern states, outraged by Lincoln's attitude toward slavery, had left the Union, setting the stage for the Civil War.

the Southern Part of Maryland" into Auburn, New York, by Harriet Tubman. The woman who had come to be known as Moses made her last rescue mission in 1860, but other efforts to free slaves continued apace.

Former slave Harriet Jacobs, one of the nation's 487,970 free blacks, published her autobiographical book, *Incidents in the Life of a Slave Girl*, in 1861. Her aim, said the author, was to "arouse the women of the North to a realizing sense of two millions of women at the South, still in bondage." Jacobs wrote about her desire to free herself and her children from an owner who harassed her. She had finally taken refuge in her grandmother's attic, where she remained for seven years. Her owner assumed she had fled to the North, a destination she and her children did eventually reach.

Although Jacobs used the pseudonym Linda Brent, abolitionists soon recognized her as the author of *Incidents*. Novelist and reformer Lydia M. Child, who made modest editorial changes in the manuscript and wrote the preface, persuaded a small group of abolitionists to purchase the book for distribution. It was also sold, for $1 per copy, at the office of the New York Anti-Slavery Society.

By March 1861, when Abraham Lincoln arrived in Washington for his inauguration, all efforts at compromise had failed: war between the North and South appeared imminent. The South, in fact, had already threatened to secede from the Union in the event of Lincoln's election. South Carolina led the southern states out of the Union on December 20, 1861. Alabama, Florida, Georgia, Louisiana, Mississippi, and Texas followed. Four additional states joined the Confederate States of America several weeks later. But as the United States moved toward

The Stars and Bars—flag of the Confederacy—flies over Fort Sumter, South Carolina, on April 14, 1861. After a fierce, 33-hour battle, the federal garrison had surrendered to southern forces, and America was at war with itself.

war, Kansas, the scene of so much conflict and violence, joined the Union on January 29, 1861, as a free state.

Lincoln took a cautious approach in his inaugural address. He wished to assure the remaining southern states that there was no reasonable cause for anxiety. He did not consider the Union broken and promised no bloodshed or violence unless forced to resort to such measures. The North and the South, he told his audience, "are not enemies, but friends. We must not be enemies."

The following day, the president learned that the federal garrison at Fort Sumter, South Carolina, was running low on supplies, and would be out of food by April 15. The president decided to send provisions to Fort Sumter rather than order its evacuation, but he first sent a message informing South Carolina's governor of his intentions. "No effort to throw in men, arms, or ammunitions will be made," wrote Lincoln.

The Confederacy responded by demanding that Union forces abandon the fort, threatening to use force if they refused. It was too late to stop the relief effort, however, and it arrived in Charleston harbor on April 12, 1861. After much discussion with his cabinet, Confederate president Jefferson Davis announced his decision to attack Fort Sumter. "Mr. President, at this time, it is suicide, murder, and you will lose us every friend in the North," responded Confederate secretary of state Robert Toombs. "It is unnecessary," he added, "it puts us in the wrong; it is fatal."

Nevertheless, the attack on Fort Sumter began in the early hours of April 12, 1861. The Union garrison did not return fire until 7:00 A.M. The troops withstood shelling for 33 hours before their commander ordered the Stars and Stripes lowered and the men evacuated. America was at war, "testing whether that nation or any nation so conceived and so dedicated," as Lincoln would put it, could "long endure." At times during the next blood-soaked years, endurance seemed unlikely, but the United States would indeed survive, and it would flourish—richer, in the end, by the addition of a great wave of new citizens: 4 million African Americans, ready to leave centuries of slavery for a future of freedom.

FURTHER READING

Bennett, Lerone, Jr. *Before the Mayflower: A History of Black America 1619–1964.* New York: Penguin, 1988.

Cornelius, Janet Duitsman. *When I Can Read My Title Clear: Literacy, Slavery, and Religion in the Antebellum South.* Columbia: University of South Carolina Press, 1991.

Delany, Martin R. *Blake; or, the Huts of Africa: A Novel by Martin R. Delany.* Edited by Floyd J. Miller. New York: Beacon Press, 1970.

Douglass, Frederick. *My Bondage and My Freedom.* New York: Dover Publications, 1969.

Foster, Frances Smith. *Written by Herself: Literary Production by African American Women, 1746–1892.* Bloomington: Indiana University Press, 1993.

Franklin, John Hope. *From Slavery to Freedom: A History of Negro Americans.* New York: Knopf, 1987.

Gara, Larry. *The Liberty Line: The Legend of the Underground Railroad.* Lexington: University of Kentucky Press, 1961.

Hine, Darline Clark, et al. eds., *Black Women in America: An Historical Encyclopedia.* New York: Carlson Publishing, 1993.

Jacobs, Harriet. *Incidents in the Life of a Slave Girl: Written by Herself.* Edited by Jean Fagan Yellin. Cambridge: Harvard University Press, 1987.

Jakoubek, Robert E. *Harriet Beecher Stowe: Author and Abolitionist.* New York: Chelsea House, 1989.

Miller, Randall, ed. *"Dear Master": Letters of a Slave Family.* Ithaca, NY: Cornell University Press, 1978.

Quarles, Benjamin. *Black Abolitionists.* New York: Oxford University Press, 1969.

Stowe, Harriet Beecher. *Uncle Tom's Cabin; or, Life Among the Lowly.* Edited by Ann Douglass. New York: Penguin Books, 1985.

INDEX

PICTURE CREDITS

WILMA KING, associate professor of history at Michigan State University, teaches courses on African American women and the antebellum South. She edited *A Northern Woman in the Plantation South: Letters of Tryphena Blanche Holder Fox, 1856–1876* and is the author of *Africa's Progeny—America's Slaves: Children and Youth in Bondage in the Nineteenth-Century South.*

CLAYBORNE CARSON, senior consulting editor of the MILESTONES IN BLACK AMERICAN HISTORY series, is a professor of history at Stanford University. His first book, *In Struggle: SNCC and the Black Awakening of the 1960s* (1981), won the Frederick Jackson Turner Prize of the Organization of American Historians. He is the director of the Martin Luther King, Jr., Papers Project, which will publish 12 volumes of King's writings.

DARLENE CLARK HINE, senior consulting editor of the MILESTONES IN BLACK AMERICAN HISTORY series, is the John A. Hannah Professor of American History at Michigan State University. She is the author of numerous books and articles on black women's history. Her most recent work is the two-volume *Black Women in America: An Historical Encyclopedia* (1993).